Music for Voice and Classical Guitar, 1945–1996

Music for Voice and Classical Guitar, 1945–1996

AN ANNOTATED CATALOG

James F. Maroney

McFarland & Company, Inc., Publishers
Jefferson, North Carolina, and London

To the memory of my father,
whose love and support, while rarely spoken,
were always strongly felt.

British Library Cataloguing-in-Publication data are available

Library of Congress Cataloguing-in-Publication Data

Maroney, James F., 1955–
    Music for voice and classical guitar, 1945–1996: an annotated catalog /
James F. Maroney.
        p.   cm.
    Includes bibliographical references and index.
    ISBN 0-7864-0384-5 (library binding : 55# alkaline paper) ∞
    1. Songs with guitar—20th century—Bibliography.   2. Sacred songs
with guitar—20th century—Bibliography.   I. Title.
ML128.S3M37   1997
016.7832'026—DC21   97-19848
                                                                          CIP
                                                                          MN

Manufactured in the United States of America

McFarland & Company, Inc., Publishers
    Box 611, Jefferson, North Carolina 28640

Contents

Acknowledgments

I am deeply indebted to the many composers and publishers who graciously donated or loaned their music to me. This project could not have been accomplished without their invaluable assistance. I am grateful to Dr. Jan Prokop for her advice in the initial stages of this endeavor. Lastly, I wish to thank my wife, Marina, for her love, encouragement, and seemingly infinite patience.

Introduction

Renowned guitarist Julian Bream once described his instrument as "*the most beautiful accompaniment to the voice.*" Contemporary composers apparently share a similar viewpoint, for there has been an ever-growing output of art songs with classical guitar since 1945. Indeed, many of the twentieth century's finest composers—Dominick Argento, Milton Babbitt, Lennox Berkeley, Benjamin Britten, Mario Castelnuovo-Tedesco, Peter Maxwell-Davies, Thea Musgrave, Daniel Pinkham, Joaquin Rodrigo, Michael Tippett, William Walton, and Charles Wuorinen—have made notable contributions to the medium. However, until now the genre has been poorly documented in both guitar and vocal music sources.

The purpose of this book is to provide musicians and teachers with an annotated catalog of music written from 1945 through 1996 expressly for the duo of solo voice and classical guitar, examining the repertoire's qualities primarily in terms of vocal performance and pedagogical use. Criteria for inclusion are as follows:

1. The composition must have been written so as to allow performance by one singer and one guitarist. Works featuring additional performers were included only if those performers were explicitly cited as being an optional alternative.

2. The work must have been written during the period of 1945 through 1996. New arrangements of pre–1945 works were acceptable provided the piece was altered to incorporate aspects of modern classical music composition and performance practice, including contemporary chordal/harmonic structures, atonality, extended vocal techniques, and expanded performance requirements for the guitar.

3. The musical notation for the guitar could not consist solely of chord symbols or other devices exclusively derived from popular music.

4. Any composition featuring a guitar part arranged from a different instrument (e.g., piano) was acceptable only if the transcription was prepared or authorized by the composer.

1

Using these criteria, 576 compositions were obtained through publishers, composers, contemporary music organizations, and libraries. It is hoped that this book will promote greater awareness and more frequent performances of these fine works.

I

Historical Background

Today the guitar is unquestionably the predominant plucked instrument in Western music. However, it did not achieve its position of preeminence until the end of the eighteenth century (Turnbull & Heck, 1980, p. 835). Prior to then, the lute and its Spanish counterpart, the vihuela, enjoyed much popularity, and the quantity and quality of their repertories in the Renaissance and Baroque eras far exceeded that of the guitar. In fact, songs accompanied by those two instruments represent a significant aspect of sixteenth- and seventeenth-century song (Chew, 1980, p. 516).

The histories of all three instruments are very much intertwined. Early forms of the guitar directly influenced the construction of the vihuela. Furthermore, the playing techniques of the lute and vihuela eventually affected guitar performance practice, and their music would later be integrated into the modern classical guitar repertoire. Therefore, in order to fully appreciate the history of music for voice and guitar, it is necessary to examine the relationships of all three instruments to the voice.

THE MIDDLE AGES TO
THE MID–FOURTEENTH CENTURY

Prior to the Renaissance, information concerning the lute or guitar as accompaniment to the voice is scant. However, existing visual evidence suggests that the medium was not uncommon. Various pages from the ninth-century *Carolingian Psalter* contain drawings showing singers accompanied by a lute- or guitar-like instrument (Bellow, 1970, p. 30), and a similar group of instruments is seen on a page from the manuscript *Commentarius Super Apocalypsum*, dated 926 A.D., in consort with an ensemble of vocalists (Bellow, 1970, p. 35).

Troubadours, the itinerate poet-musicians of twelfth- and thirteenth-century southern France, sang their songs to instrumental accompaniment. Quite often their instrument of choice was some early form of lute or guitar, favored because of its versatility and portability (Bellow, 1970, p. 43). The troubadour movement spread to northern France, Germany and Spain, with the latter producing several singers noted particularly for their playing of these instruments. They include Jot Aben, a twelfth-century native of Valencia, and Juan Nadal, mentioned in a 1389 Valencian document. Also noted was Alonso de Carrion, a jongleur from the fifteenth century who often accompanied troubadours who were unable to play an instrument (Bellow, 1970, p. 46).

THE LATE FOURTEENTH CENTURY
TO THE SEVENTEENTH CENTURY

The Lute

The use of the European lute was evident by the 1270s (Wachsmann, McKinnon, Harwood, & Poulton, 1980, p. 357). It was derived from the Arabic lute, which was introduced into Europe by the Moors during their conquest and occupation of Spain from 711 to 1492 (Wachsmann et al., 1980, p. 346). Distinguished by its pear-shaped soundbox and sideless, bowl-like back, the lute would become the principal plucked instrument in Europe until the late eighteenth century. Beginning in the late fourteenth century, it was commonly used in *chanson* by composers such as Machaut (and later, Dufay and Josquin, among others) to play all parts other than the sung melody (Hurley, 1989c, p. 40).

After the development of the first movable type music printing press in the late fifteenth century, books featuring lute music became increasingly common. Some examples of published lute-songs of the time include the *Tenori e contrabassi intabulati col sopran in canto figurato per cantar e sonar col lauto* (*Libro primo*, 1509; *Libro secundo*, 1511) by lutenist Franciscus Bossinensis (Wachsmann et al., 1980, p. 358); Arnolt Schlick's 1512 *Tabulaturen etlicher Lobgesang und Liedlein* (Wachsmann et al., 1980, p. 359); and an undated (*c.* 1520s) collection of early *frottole* by Marchetto Cara and Bartolomeo Tromboncino (Wachsmann et al., 1980, p. 358).

By the time of the late Renaissance, the lute was the most commonly used instrument in Europe and England, especially among the ruling class (Bellow, 1970, p. 56). Thus a vast and significant repertory for the instrument grew during that time, second only to those of organ and harpsichord (Apel, 1969, p. 493).

One notable form of music for voice(s) and lute that developed in this period was the French *air de cour*. Having evolved from the simple, chordal *vaul de ville* songs of the mid-sixteenth century (Apel, 1969, pp. 895–896; Chew, 1980, p. 515), airs de cour were short strophic compositions, sometimes with a refrain, in syllabic style and binary form. The texts often consisted of love poems, some of them employing the rhythmically asymmetrical technique of *vers mesuré* (Hurley, 1989c, p. 42). Like the *da capo* aria of that time, the repetition of each section was often freely ornamented by the singer (Apel, 1969, p. 25). The air de cour first appeared in print in Adrian Le Roy and Robert Ballard's 1571 *Livre d'airs de cour*, and remained popular in France throughout much of the 17th century, aided by the contributions of composers such as Pierre Guédron, Antoine Boësset, Jean de Cambefort, and Etienne Moulinié (Randel, 1986, p. 26).

The lute-song is known to have been cultivated in England as early as the reign of Henry VIII (1491–1547), yet little music of that time has survived (Chew, 1980, p. 516). In the late sixteenth and early seventeenth centuries, the *ayre* proved to be a notable English contribution to this medium. Derived from the French air de cour, ayres covered a wide range of moods, from serious songs, often through-composed, to cheerful, light-hearted pieces that were frequently strophic. The earliest known publication of ayres was *The first Booke of Songs or Ayres* by John Dowland in 1597 (Randel, 1986, p. 63). Over the next 25 years roughly 30 collections would be published, culminating with John Attay's 1622 *First Book of Ayres* (Wachsmann et al., 1980, p. 362). Other prominent composers of this genre include Thomas Campion, Henry Purcell, and Thomas Morley (Hurley, 1989c, p. 41).

While the air de cour and ayre were the most significant forms of lute-songs, other contributions of that time are noteworthy. The Italian *frottola* was a light, secular, homophonic song primarily of the late fifteenth and early sixteenth centuries. The melody was usually the highest of its four parts, and although they were frequently performed as part songs, the practice of singing frottole as solos with lute or other instrumental accompaniment was common (Chew, 1980, p. 516). There also survives a body of two-part arrangements of songs by sixteenth-century German lutenists in which the melody could have been sung. However, the absence of any published collections of lute-songs from Germany indicates that the medium was probably not as widely accepted there as in other European countries (Chew, 1980, p. 516).

The lute remained in active use until the late eighteenth century; yet from all accounts it seems that its appeal after the early 1600s lay primarily in solo or instrumental ensemble works. One notable exception was in the vocal works of Handel, who used the lute as an obbligato instrument in various arias, such as "The soft complaining flute" in his *Ode for St Cecilia's Day* (1739), and "Due bell'aline" from his 1741 *Deidamia* (Wachsmann et al., 1980, p. 363).

The Vihuela

In sixteenth-century Spain, the lute's popularity was undermined by its close association with the Moors, who, until shortly before that time, had oppressively dominated the country for centuries. However, the Spanish aristocracy admired the music written for the lute and sought an alternative instrument on which that music could be performed satisfactorily. Initially, they turned to the popular Spanish *guitarra*, with its flat back and soundbox and curved sides (the qualities which distinguish the guitar family). The four double strings of the guitarra, however, were insufficient to play the polyphonic music written for the six-course lute. Furthermore, the aristocracy wanted an instrument that would not be associated with the common class. Subsequently, the guitarra was enlarged and given two additional courses of double strings, and came to be known as the vihuela (Bellow, 1970, p. 56). With the refinement of the vihuela came a golden age of Spanish song (Hurley, 1989c, p. 41). However, by the end of the sixteenth century the vihuela's popularity had rapidly and irreversibly declined, owing to the increasing prominence of four- and five-course guitars (Poulton, 1980, p. 759).

One notable song form of that time was the *villancico*, often character-ized by a love poem of great intensity, consisting of several stanzas linked to a refrain (Apel, 1969, p. 902). Many villancicos were written for solo voice and vihuela, yet they were also composed for multiple a cappella voices and then later arranged for the former (Poulton, 1980, p. 760). A number of villancicos are considered to be outstanding for their sophistication and elegance, and "indeed might be considered the earliest examples of song in the modern sense of the word" (Apel, 1969, p. 903). Leading contributors to this genre included Luis de Milán, Miguel de Fuenllana, and Alonso Mudarra (Randel, 1986, p. 912).

Just as significant as the villancico was the *romance*, featuring a poem dealing with historical subjects, often incidents in the battle of Spain against the Moors or the adventures of the knights of Charlemagne (Poulton, 1980, p. 760). Romances first appeared in Luis de Milán's *Libro de música de vihuela de mano intitulado El maestro* (1536) and remained popular until the last known vihuela publication, Esteban Daza's 1576 *El Parnaso* (Bellow, 1970, p. 63). Other important composers of romances were Luis de Narváez and Alonso Mudarra (Apel, 1969, p. 736).

Additional songs in wide variety were frequently arranged for solo voice and vihuela in sixteenth-century Spain, among them *madrigales*, Italian *sone-tos*, chansons by Verdelot and others, settings of *coplas* by Boscán and Gar-cilaso and of poems by Petrarch, and *ensaladas* (Poulton, 1980, p. 760).

The Guitar

Current knowledge concerning the guitar's history prior to the Renais-sance is largely conjecture. However, the appearance of a small four-course guitar in fifteenth-century Italy, Spain, and France is amply documented (Turnbull & Heck, 1980, p. 828). Because it was ill-suited to polyphony com-pared to the six-course lute and vihuela, the four-course guitar was most often accorded music featuring chordal textures or simple contrapuntal movement (Turnbull & Heck, 1980, p. 830). Consequently, it was deemed less significant than, and subservient to, the lute and vihuela in Italy and Spain. However, it was so popular in France that one author there said the lute had almost been forgotten (Turnbull & Heck, 1980, p. 830). It is not surprising, then, that much of the significant music written for the four-course guitar was published in France. Little mention is made of songs with that instrument except for several books published in Paris by Adrian Le Roy between 1551 and 1555, containing works by Le Roy and Grégoire Brayssing (Bellow, 1970, p. 67).

To overcome the four-course guitar's technical limitations, an extra double-string course was added during the mid-sixteenth century in Spain. This new five-course instrument became known as the *guitarra española*. It was widely used throughout Europe during the late sixteenth and throughout the seventeenth century, and was partly responsible for the lute's decline. Because it often consisted solely of chordal accompaniment, the music for the guitarra española was much easier to play than the increasingly sophisticated and difficult works written for the lute during that time. Thus the guitarra española enjoyed greater popular appeal (Apel, 1969, p. 362).

Despite its Spanish origins, interest in the guitarra española was perhaps strongest in early seventeenth-century Italy, which produced many exceptional performers and the greatest amount of music written for the instrument (Bellow, 1970, p. 121). Steffano Landi, a noted opera composer in Rome during that time, wrote a group of six songs with guitar accompaniment (Bellow, 1970, p. 115). The connection between Italian singers and guitarists is evident based on Scipione Cerreto's early seventeenth-century *Della practica musica vocale e strumentale*, a book devoted to that topic (Bellow, 1970, p. 116). Orazio Tarditi, another opera composer and the organist at St. Michael's Church in Murano, frequently advocated the use of the guitar in church singing (Bellow, 1970, p. 115). After the early seventeenth century, little music for voice and five-course guitar is noted, except for an early cantata by Handel entitled *No se emendera jamas (cantata spagñuola)* for soprano, guitar, and continuo (Bellow, 1970, p. 126).

THE EIGHTEENTH CENTURY
AND EARLY NINETEENTH CENTURY

During the Eighteenth century, art song became a medium largely for solo song with keyboard accompaniment. This trend began as early as the middle of the seventeenth century with the harpsichord as the initial instrument of choice, and reached full fruition in the 1800s, with the piano reigning. However, the guitar would never be completely superseded (Chew, 1980, pp. 517–518).

By the last decades of the 1700s, the transition was made from the five-course guitarra española to an instrument with six single strings. Few songs were written for this new guitar in the first few decades of its emergence. Several known groups include a sizable body published in Paris by French virtuoso Trille Labarre (Bellow, 1970, p. 134), and a collection by the Swedish composer Carl Michael Bellman (Hurley, 1990a, p. 47).

However, the first half of the nineteenth century saw a significant increase of songs with guitar accompaniment (Hurley, 1990a, p. 44), aided by the instrument's widening popularity in northern Europe (Bellow, 1970, p. 127) and the fact that it was considered accessible to the masses. Hence, the majority of guitar music in the early nineteenth century—accompanimental or solo—was rather simplistic, often consisting of arpeggios and broken chords (Turnbull & Heck, 1980, p. 837), in order to appeal to the widely varying capabilities of amateur guitarists.

Interest in the guitar during that time was most evident in Vienna, owing largely to the efforts and influence of performer Mauro Giuliani, who gave some of the earliest concerts in which the guitar as a solo instrument was the main attraction (Bellow, 1970, pp. 158-159). Giuliani also wrote a vast amount of music for the guitar, including works with other instruments, orchestra, and voice. In the latter category he composed 174 songs in three languages (Hurley, 1989a, p. 33), including his *Sei Ariette* (Op. 95), *Sei Cavatine* (Op. 39) and *Sechs Lieder* (Op. 89) (Hurley, 1990a, p. 46).

This Viennese guitar school influenced several renowned composers residing in the city at that time. Franz Schubert wrote many songs with guitar (Hurley, 1990a, p. 46); approximately 20 of them were published during his lifetime (Bellow, 1970, pp. 160-161). Carl Maria von Weber played the guitar (Bellow, 1970, p. 176) and composed 90 or more songs for it (Appleby, 1951, p. 193). He also featured the guitar in arias from his operas *Abu Hassan* and *Oberon*. The surge in popularity of the guitar in Vienna also prompted numerous transcriptions, including songs by Beethoven and Haydn (Hurley, 1990a, p. 47).

In other parts of Europe the guitar was gaining greater acceptance. Rossini used it in certain operas, as did Verdi (Bellow, 1970, p. 172). Danish composers A.P. Bergreen, Henrik Rung (Hurley, 1990a, p. 47), and Peter Schall (Bellow, 1970, p. 127) were writing songs for the instrument, as were prominent composers from Spain, notably Fernando Sor and Federico Moretti. In addition to having written many songs, Sor is credited with introducing the new six-string guitar to England in 1809, heralding a golden age of popularity there that lasted roughly 30 years. During that time, many guitarists came from Europe to teach the art of singing to guitar accompaniment (Appleby, 1951, p. 193). The medium was so popular that many early nineteenth-century English ballads were transcribed for guitar from their original piano or orchestral accompaniment (Hurley, 1990a, p. 45), and a catalog issued by S. Chappel during that period contained over 200 guitar songs, most of which were probably transcriptions (Appleby, 1951, p. 193).

The popularity of the guitar in song is also documented in nineteenth-century America. Stephen Foster took 19 of his songs originally written for piano and arranged the accompaniments for guitar (Hurley, 1990a, p. 45). Holdings of mid–1800 American music in the Library of Congress reveal a significant body for voice and guitar, consisting exclusively of transcriptions of popular songs with piano.

THE LATE NINETEENTH CENTURY
AND TWENTIETH CENTURY

The early nineteenth-century six-string guitar evolved in the late 1800s to its larger, standardized contemporary design. Not coincidentally, the development of its modern playing technique began in the same era. At the onset of this period, the guitar possessed an insignificant repertory, consisting largely of transcriptions of pieces for lute, vihuela, and bowed and keyboard instruments (Turnbull & Heck, 1980, p. 838).

As the 20th century progressed, however, the literature for the guitar grew dramatically. Much of this can be attributed to contributions by composers who were not guitarists. Such a trend ran contrary to the long-standing tradition of guitarist-composers, and led to compositions that were not constrained by traditional notions of the guitar's capabilities. Consequently, the twentieth century has witnessed a significant increase of works of considerable stature for guitar.

Despite its growth during the first half of the twentieth century, the serious repertory for guitar was devoid of ensemble compositions, especially those with voice. Given the frequently subservient, accompanimental status accorded to the instrument in previous eras, it seems logical that, in order to elevate its standing, the guitar's newer repertory would have to be markedly dissociated from that of its past. Only in such a manner could the instrument be allowed to reach its full potential.

By the second half of the twentieth century, composers and performers felt that this potential was being realized. Since 1945, there has been much renewed interest in the medium of voice and guitar, with hundreds of compositions being written by many renowned composers. These works range from short, simple pieces to challenging and substantial song cycles. Many seek to exploit the full potential of both instruments and are strikingly original. Judging by the ever-increasing quantity of this music, these pieces have also proved musically satisfying for composer, performer, and audience. These qualities likely explain why the current resurgence in interest shows no signs of abating.

II

Statistical and Pedagogical Observations

STATISTICS

Five hundred seventy-six compositions for voice and classical guitar written from 1945 through 1996 were obtained and annotated. An examination of the music yields significant statistics about the medium in terms of composers, difficulty level, voice type, languages, and dates.

Composers

Three hundred forty-five contemporary composers are represented, comprising 316 males and 29 females. The men produced 529 pieces, yielding an average of 1.67 pieces per person, while the women contributed 47 works for an average of 1.62 compositions each.

Difficulty Levels of the Music

The difficulty of each work is denoted by one of four levels: Easy, Medium, Difficult, and Very Difficult. Table 1 shows the distribution of the works into the four categories.

Roughly two-thirds of the music lies in the two intermediate levels (66 percent). The extreme categories of Easy and Very Difficult account for only a little more than one third (34 percent). It is therefore evident that the technical demands of most of the repertoire are compatible with the capabilities of many singers and guitarists.

Table 1
The number of works in each difficulty level.

Difficulty Level	Number of Works	Incidence
Easy	89	15%
Medium	171	30%
Difficult	206	36%
Very Difficult (VD)	110	19%

The two most demanding levels comprise a total of almost 55 percent of the music, in comparison to the 45 percent sum of the two least difficult. Furthermore, the Easy category contains the smallest percentage of works (15 percent). The relatively few compositions appropriate for beginning singers may explain in part why the genre has yet to gain the recognition it deserves. By the time a singer acquires the technical ability and musical sophistication to pursue much of this repertory, certain preconceived ideas may already exist (e.g., that the piano is more appropriate for accompaniment than other instruments) that could inhibit the study and performance of songs with classical guitar.

Although many composers are writing works of significant challenge, there appears to be a need for more compositions which can be performed by beginning vocalists. Such pieces are necessary to foster interest in the medium during a singer's early, perhaps more impressionable years.

Available Works for Various Voice Types

In many cases the voice type for a work was noted on the musical score. Common classifications included soprano, mezzo, alto, tenor, baritone, bass, high, medium, low, female, and male. If no voice type was noted, it was determined by this author based on the composition's pitch range and tessitura, and designated as high, medium, or low. A more specific classification was given only when information was explicit.

Table 2 illustrates the number of works available for the voice types of soprano, mezzo, alto, tenor, baritone, and bass.

Table 2
The number of works in each voice type.

Voice Type	Number of Works	Incidence
Soprano	281	49%
Mezzo	234	41%
Alto	60	10%
Tenor	230	40%
Baritone	215	37%
Bass	47	8%

Note. Other classifications were merged as follows: **high**—soprano, tenor; **medium**—mezzo, baritone; **low**—alto, bass; **female**—soprano, mezzo, alto; **male**—tenor, baritone, bass; **any voice range**—all voice types; **various**—all voice types.

Table 2 reveals that the most music—virtually half (49 percent)—was written for soprano, followed by mezzo with 41 percent. This finding closely matches a study by Hunt (1992) of contemporary voice and percussion music, which likewise noted the dominance of female voices. Table 2 also shows that higher voices of either gender tend to be preferred over lower voice types. Sopranos and tenors had the highest percentages in their respective genders, averaging about 45 percent. The two medium voice types (mezzos and baritones) occupied the middle percentages, and yielded an average of roughly 39 percent. A relative lack of music written specifically for low voices is evident, given the average of only 9 percent for works for altos and basses.

Perhaps one reason for the preference of higher voices is that they generally possess a more flexible and agile technique than their lower counterparts. Given the technical challenges of much twentieth-century vocal music, such dexterity would be advantageous. Table 3, showing the number of works in each difficulty rating by voice type, supports this idea.

Table 3
The number of works in each
difficulty rating for each voice type.

	Number of Works				*Percentage of Voice Type's Repertoire*			
Voice	*VD*	*D*	*M*	*E*	*VD*	*D*	*M*	*E*
Soprano	56	117	77	31	20%	42%	27%	11%
Mezzo	28	76	74	56	12%	32%	32%	24%
Alto	6	25	14	5	10%	42%	23%	25%
Tenor	32	91	74	33	14%	40%	32%	14%
Baritone	26	63	74	52	12%	29%	35%	24%
Bass	3	21	11	12	6%	45%	23%	26%

VD = very difficult; D = difficult; M = medium; E = easy; see page 22.

Table 3 reveals that sopranos and tenors have a higher percentage of pieces in the Very Difficult classification than the other voice types, followed by the medium and low voices respectively. They also possess the lowest percentages in the Easy category; an inverse relationship can be noted in the lower voices.

Available Works for Various Languages

Twenty-six different languages were found in the music. They are presented in Table 4, and are also listed—with the exception of English—in the General Index for further reference.

Table 4
The languages used in the music.

Language	Number of Works	Incidence
Arabic	1	.2%
Bulgarian	1	.2%
Catalonian	2	.3%
Czech	1	.2%
Danish	16	2.8%
Dutch	6	1.0%
English	234	40.6%
Finnish	9	1.6%
French	29	5.0%
Friulian	1	.2%
German	100	17.4%
Hungarian	2	.3%
Icelandic	2	.3%
Italian	14	2.4%
Japanese	3	.5%
Latin	8	1.4%
Norwegian	7	1.2%
Polish	3	.5%
Portuguese	4	.7%
Rumanian	1	.2%
Russian	1	.2%
Spanish	85	14.8%
Swedish	28	4.9%
Welsh	1	.2%
Yiddish	4	.7%
Zulu	1	.2%
Phonetic sounds	8	1.4%
No language or sounds specified	11	1.9%

English was the most widely used language with 234 entries, comprising close to 41 percent of the music, followed by German and Spanish with 100 and 85 pieces respectively. Combining the works of the six languages in which classically trained singers are expected to be proficient (English, Italian, German, French, Spanish, and Latin) produces a total of 470 pieces, consisting of almost 82 percent of the music. This figure confirms that, in terms of language accessibility, much of this repertory can readily be pursued by most singers. There are also numerous works in the languages of Northern Europe—

_...쑈ish (28), Danish (16), Finnish (9), Norwegian (7), and Dutch (6)— thereby offering singers ample opportunity to perform songs in languages considered less traditional in vocal study. The relatively small number of pieces utilizing phonetic sounds (8) implies that perhaps many composers have yet to readily embrace this unconventional aspect of twentieth-century composition in the music. Lastly, the data in Table 4 indicate that singers who pursue this repertory have many languages from which to choose. They should thus be strongly encouraged to investigate and perform contemporary music for voice and classical guitar.

Dates of Composition

Of the 576 works, 392 yielded clear evidence as to their specific year of composition. Table 5 shows the number of works written in each decade, and indicates that the average number of pieces composed per year has increased steadily.

Table 5
The number of works composed in each decade.

Decade	Number of Works	Average per Year
1945-1949	6	1.2
1950-1959	21	2.1
1960-1969	58	5.8
1970-1979	86	8.6
1980-1989	129	12.9
1990-1996	93	13.3

PEDAGOGY

The late twentieth century has witnessed significant developments in terms of musical composition. Post–World War II composers have developed and adopted a wide array of new approaches to music, such as serialism, aleatoricism, and minimalism. Other styles normally not associated with Western art music such as popular music (e.g., jazz and rock) and music of other cultures (e.g., Africa and the Orient) have also been influential, as have visual aspects of the theater. Much of this new music is quite complex in its use of pitch, rhythm, dynamics, timbre, and form.

Contemporary vocal music often places great technical demands on the performer. A singer may be required to execute highly disjunct phrases containing unusual intervals and intricate rhythms, to perform in outermost pitch ranges at extreme dynamic levels, or to produce a wide variety of unusual tone colors and sounds.

In order to facilitate the performance of this music, composers have developed new systems of musical notation. Scores featuring graphs, pictures, and numerous other new devices are becoming increasingly commonplace.

However, most of what is performed and studied in the vocal repertory of Western art music consists of works from the eighteenth and nineteenth centuries. This music is generally perceived as the embodiment of "traditional" Western practice in its use of tonality, harmony, melody, rhythm, pitch range, dynamics, timbre, form, and notation. Consequently, many singers and teachers are unfamiliar with modern music notation and performance practice.

An examination of the music in this book provided pertinent information about its use of late twentieth-century compositional techniques that differ notably from practices of the previous two centuries. The aspects to be considered will be those most likely to influence singers and teachers in selecting works in the modern repertoire. They include expanded pitch range, extended vocal techniques, atonality, expanded use of rhythm, and unusual notational devices.

Expanded Pitch Range

In Western art music, pitch range is of vital concern to singers. The classifications commonly used to categorize vocalists (soprano, alto, tenor, bass, etc.) are largely based on the span of pitches that a person is comfortably capable of singing. Similarly, the range of a composition is one of the primary factors in determining if a vocalist can perform a piece. The musically functional range of many singers is considered to be roughly two octaves (Apel, 1969, p. 920; Vennard, 1967, p. 79). Works from before the twentieth century generally stayed well within that boundary (although exceptions do exist). In contrast, a distinctive trait of much contemporary music is the use of vocal ranges exceeding two octaves (Apel, 1969, p. 920). Therefore, an examination of pitch range is an important consideration for singers and teachers when selecting works from the modern repertory.

Of the 576 works listed, 569 yielded clear evidence as to the range of pitches which were to be sung. The narrowest range found for an entire piece was from A3 to C4, a minor third, in the song *Nunca Como Mi Querer* by Ismael Moreno. The largest consisted of three octaves and a minor second, from Cᵇ3 to C6, in Alois Broder's *14 Haiku*, the only piece in the music to equal or exceed a three-octave span. The lowest single pitch was C2, in the *Sonnetina #6* by Leonard Lehrman, while the highest was Eᵇ6, in Siegfried Behrend's *Yo Lo Vi*.

Table 6 shows the number of works in three classifications of pitch range.

The table reveals that a significant majority of the music—close to 87 percent—contains a pitch range of one to two octaves. Given that most singers of Western art music aspire to attain a minimum of two octaves of singing voice, these data demonstrate that most of the music is within the capabilities of many vocalists.

Table 6
The distribution of works among pitch ranges.

Pitch Range	Number of Works	Incidence
Less than 1 octave	19	3%
1-2 octaves	499	87%
Greater than 2 octaves	49	9%
No indication	9	1%

Nevertheless, the presence of works whose span exceeds two octaves implies that a number of composers consider the genre suitable for this facet of twentieth-century composition. In order to avail themselves of as much of the modern repertory as possible, singers must strive to expand their pitch range to its fullest extent. Voice teachers should encourage this (as many already do), and likewise should provide students with greater exposure to contemporary works that incorporate a very wide pitch range.

Atonality

Tonality can be defined as the preference of a single pitch in a piece, making it the tonal center to which all other tones are related (Apel, 1969, p. 855). In Western music during the eighteenth and nineteenth centuries, tonality was realized through a system based primarily on consonant harmonic function, which in turn influenced melody and melodic movement. Although the system evolved greatly, one of its main tenets was that consonance would largely prevail over dissonance in order to preserve harmonic clarity. Consequently, the pitches within the melody of a composition generally consisted of tones common to the harmony, thereby preserving consonance and at the same time reinforcing the harmonic and tonal structure of the piece. As such, the accurate singing of pitches was often facilitated by the limited choice of tones which agreed with the harmonic scheme. In addition, the melodic pitches frequently yielded implications as to a composition's chordal make-up.

However, composers in the twentieth century have written much music in which tonality is increasingly elusive, and in many instances banished altogether. Atonality allows and encourages the widespread use of nontraditional chord structures, commonly resulting in numerous dissonances and a lack of conventional harmonic function. Singers of atonal music must possess the ability to produce pitches which are often dissonant to the other notes being performed, or components of chords that are structurally unusual. In addition, the sung pitches frequently do not imply any harmonic construct.

Therefore, the singing of atonal music contrasts significantly in many ways with the performance of tonal compositions, and is one of the most pronounced challenges facing a singer in the modern repertoire. Of the 576 works listed, a total of 181 pieces (31 percent) utilized atonality, making it the most widely employed of the twentieth-century techniques discussed here. This finding suggests that while most of the music is written in a tonal idiom, many composers nevertheless view atonality as appropriate for voice and classical guitar. The sizable number of atonal works also implies that singers are expected to be competent in executing such music. Higher standards of ear training should be encouraged for vocalists in order to develop the acute sense of pitch discrimination necessary to perform these works. Furthermore, singers and voice teachers need to pursue contemporary atonal music more frequently to gain greater command of its difficulties. Those unable to meet these demands will be denied access to the experiences offered by this significant portion of the music.

Expanded Use of Rhythm

Rhythm refers to the movement of music in time (Apel, 1969, p. 729). In Western music from approximately 1600 to 1900 the type most used was isometric rhythm, in which all time values are derived arithmetically from a beat. The measures in isometric rhythms receive the strongest accent on the first beat and are equal to each other. As a result, isometric rhythms generally possess regularity and strong mathematical relationships, enabling trained musicians to respond almost intuitively to many of its numerous components.

Nonetheless, the use of isometric rhythms is considered restrictive by many twentieth-century composers. As a result, much contemporary music explores rhythmic devices such as ametricality, multimetricality, microrhythms, and approximate durations (Hunt, 1992, p. 403). Since these approaches largely run contrary to the precepts of isometricism, many performers are unaccustomed to them, and consequently find much contemporary music to be challenging.

Examination of the music finds that 24 percent (184) of the compositions utilize at least one of the aforementioned rhythmic devices. Therefore, in order to perform as much of the repertory as possible, singers and teachers should strive to enhance performance capabilities by incorporating the study of contemporary rhythm techniques and pieces containing them into the vocal regimen. Only in this manner will singers develop the rhythmic skills necessary to negotiate a considerable portion of this music.

Extended Vocal Techniques

Prior to the twentieth century, singing in Western music consisted almost exclusively of the vocalization of words to pitches from traditional Western scales. However, modern composers often use other types of vocal sounds in their music, thus expanding the role and expectations of contemporary singing. These new facets of vocal technique include whispering, speaking, sprech-stimme, glissando, improvisation, distinct vocal registers (e.g., falsetto), quarter tones, approximate pitches, phonetic sounds, and theatrical techniques (Hunt, 1992, p. 397).

An examination of the music reveals that 121 works (16 percent of the music) incorporate one or more aspects of extended vocal technique, of which the most common were speaking, sprechstimme, and glissando. The fact that nearly one-sixth of this genre employs such practices signifies that this is an integral aspect of contemporary music which should be considered seriously. Vocalists and teachers studying twentieth-century music for voice and classical guitar will need to educate themselves concerning the use of nontraditional singing techniques; otherwise a sizable number of works will be inaccessible to them.

Unusual Notational Devices

Since the early seventeenth century, notation of Western art music has generally consisted of notes being placed on a five-line staff, with the shape of the note determining its relative duration, and its pitch judged by its vertical position on the staff in conjunction with a clef. Other symbols include time and key signatures, accidentals, and marks for dynamics, tempo, and expression.

In the twentieth century, composers began developing new symbols and systems of musical notation to better convey their increasingly nontraditional musical demands. Graphs, pictures and many other types of unconventional symbols have become increasingly commonplace.

Fifty-four works, consisting of 9 percent of the music, were found to contain unusual notational devices. They ranged from signs derived from traditional music sources (such as isolated fragments of musical staffs), to those of nonmusical origin (such as a balloon and a cigarette with an arrow to indicate the latter being exploded by the former), to symbols that were completely original and often ambiguous (as in the abstract pictorial score of Roman Hauben-stock-Ramati's *La Sonnambula*). The somewhat low percentage of works containing such devices demonstrates that many composers have yet to readily embrace their use, perhaps owing to the lack of standardization of new notation (Hunt, 1992, p. 414). Whatever the cause(s) for their relative absence, the current role of unusual notation devices in the music for voice and classical guitar seems to be less significant than the use of other contemporary techniques.

Collective Use of Nontraditional Devices in the Music

An examination of the music indicates that 283 compositions (49 percent) utilize at least one of the five noted aspects of contemporary composition. Table 7 shows the number of nontraditional devices used in each work. It reveals that the quantity of such devices in a piece bears an inverse relationship to the number of works. Of the 283 applicable compositions, slightly less than one half (46 percent) employ no more than one, while those featuring all five represent less than 5 percent. The data show that singers and teachers inexperienced with unconventional practices have access to a sizable body of pieces that can allow gradual assimilation of these devices.

Table 7
The number of nontraditional devices used per composition.

Amount of Devices Employed	*Number of Works*	*Incidence*
1	131	23%
2	63	11%
3	47	8%
4	29	5%
5	13	2%

Lastly, the significant percentage of compositions utilizing new techniques confirms that such works are an integral part of the contemporary repertoire for voice and classical guitar, and therefore should be studied in order to acquire a comprehensive understanding of the music.

III

Catalog of Works

The compositions are presented in alphabetical order first by composer, and second by title (articles such as *a*, *an*, and *the* and their foreign language eqivalents are not considered in the alphabetical sorting). To look for works by language, voice range, difficulty, title, publisher, author/poet, and classification, please refer to the indexes at the end of the book.

The following sample entry provides an explanation of the format:

[1]243 [2]**Henze,** Hans Werner. [3]*Drei Fragmente nach Hölderlin* [4](German). [5]1958/c1960 [6]Schott ED 4886. [7]Text by Friedrich Hölderlin from *In Lieblicher Bläue.* [8]Tenor [9]A#2-A4/E♭3-G4. [10]*VD.* [11]Cycle of three songs (12'), from Henze's *Kammermusik 1958.* Atonal with highly disjunct melodic motion. Many very long, legato vocal phrases with difficult and rapid rhythms. Dynamic levels of pianissimo and softer on high notes are common. Highly challenging guitar part.

[1]*Entry Number*: Indicates entry's position in catalog. Indexes refer to this number.

[2]*Composer*: The last name of the composer is given first, followed by the first name and, when available, other names or initials.

[3]*Title*: The title of the work as it appears on the musical score.

[4]*Language*: This indicates the language in which the work is to be sung. If a language is not specified, either the work uses phonetic sounds exclusively, or else no language information was available.

[5]*Composed/Copyright dates*: The year in which the piece was written is given, along with its copyright date (preceded by "c"). If an entry is blank, the date was unavailable. To verify that a work was written after 1945, information was obtained from the composer, publisher, biographical sources, or analysis of the score. Despite these endeavors, there remained three works whose post–1945 creation could satisfactorily be neither proved nor disproved. To avoid the risk of wrongly excluding any piece, these works were included and indicated by an asterisk.

[6]*Publisher* and *Catalog number*: For all published works, a key name is given for the publisher; Appendix A provides further information. If the word *composer* is listed, then the score is obtainable through the composer. Please refer to Appendix B for composers' addresses. An italicized entry denotes

music from a periodical, giving the name and volume number. The name of a library indicates the source of an unpublished work whose composer could not be contacted. The work's catalog number, if provided, follows the publisher's key name.

[7]*Author* and *Text source*: The name of the author of the text is provided whenever possible. "Text by various authors" indicates two or more known contributors. Text sources can include books, specific poems, and liturgical sources. If an author or text source is not specified, no conclusive information was available.

[8]*Voice type*: This denotes the type of voice required to sing the piece, as indicated on the score. When such information was unavailable, this determination was made by the music's tessitura, and designated as either *high*, *medium*, or *low*. More specific classifications (e.g., *soprano, tenor, female, male*, etc.) were given only when information was explicit. For collections (see *Comments* below) that contain songs of different tessitura, the term *various* is used.

[9]*Range/Tessitura*: The former specifies the lowest and highest notes of the voice part, while the latter indicates the predominant pitch range. Pitches were designated according to standard international acoustic terminology, with *C1* representing the lowest C on the modern piano. Each successively higher C begins a new register, and is increased by one integer (e.g., *C4* is middle C). When the *Voice type* listing is *high, medium*, or *low*, the *range* and *tessitura* are given for a female singer; the male singer's pitches for any such song are an octave lower.

[10]*Difficulty*: This refers to one of four levels of performance ability required primarily by the singer. Criteria for determining the level of difficulty generally include the work's length and degree of tonality, along with its use of melodic motion, pitch range, rhythm, and dynamics.

1. **Easy** (*E*) denotes music which contains few technical challenges and therefore is generally intended for beginning singers.

2. **Medium** (*M*) means that a work poses some moderate challenges and would likely be appropriate for a singer with one to three years of vocal instruction.

3. **Difficult** (*D*) indicates a composition in which significant technical and musical demands are placed on the singer. This music is best suited to more advanced vocalists, such as those on the upper undergraduate or graduate level of performance.

4. **Very Difficult** (*VD*) refers to highly challenging works that frequently require extreme technical demands, and which are usually reserved for singers on the graduate or professional level.

[11]*Comments*: A general discussion of several important aspects of each work. This discussion begins with the work's classification as either a song cycle, a group of songs, a collection of songs, or a single song. (See terms below.) If a work is not denoted as a *cycle, group*, or *collection*, it is a single song.

If the work consists of more than one song, the number is specified. Collections devoted solely to one composer are treated as single entries. Individual works within a collection are annotated only when several composers are featured.

Following the classification, the comment section notes the approximate duration for the song cycle, group of songs, or any single song that exceeds six minutes. The time is usually shown in terms of minutes; more precise listings are given only when such information was provided by the composer or publisher.

Technical concerns that are integral in selecting a work for study and performance are next discussed and may include the degree of tonality, extended techniques, and characteristics of the voice part, such as its use of pitch, rhythm, dynamics, and text. Although this section examines the work from a largely vocal perspective, brief comments about the guitar part are included when possible. Other aspects contributing to the work's distinction are also mentioned when applicable.

Terms often used in this catalog include:

accessible: Within the technical command of most performers.

active: A significant degree of melodic or harmonic activity occurs within a period of time. For example, a guitar part consisting of eighth-note arpeggios is more active than one comprised of half-note chords.

classical guitar: Similar in design to the folk guitar, the classical version has a wider neck. In general, the latter uses strings of nylon (the lower strings have gold or silver casings), while the former uses plastic or steel strings. The playing technique of the classical guitar usually requires greater individual finger independence in the right hand, and the plucking of strings with the fingernails (as opposed to the use of a plectrum for the folk guitar).

collection: A set of songs in which each work was composed independently. The songs are not linked by any explicit common trait except perhaps that of composer, and they are not expected to be performed together.

course: A set of strings tuned in unison or to the octave and plucked together to obtain greater volume. To simplify terminology, a string plucked separately is also referred to as a course. For example, the sixteenth-century lute generally had 11 strings in 6 courses: G2-G3, C3-C4, F3-F4, A3-A3, D4-D4, and G4.

cycle: A set of songs specifically designed to be performed collectively in a particular sequence. Song cycles often convey a series of events or impressions, or are unified by a single mood. They are generally given artistically descriptive titles (e.g., *Halifax, 6 December 1917* or *Early One Morning*) as opposed to titles suggesting quantity (compare with **group**). Works in a group were denoted as cycles only when supportive information was explicit.

group: A collectively titled set of songs by one composer, linked by a common theme, compositional style or opus number, yet not organized in a fashion that necessitates their being performed together or in a given sequence. Such works are generally denoted by titles referring to quantity, such as *Six Haiku* or *Four Poems of Robert Graves*.

Spanish music or **Spanish folk style**: Various musical qualities commonly associated with the folk music of Spain. They include:

1. Use of the E (Phrygian) mode, with alterations of F and G (e.g., A-G#(G)-F#(F)-E), producing frequent fluctuations to major and minor.
2. Descending, parallel modal cadences (GBD to FAC to EG#B).
3. Many parallel thirds.
4. Repetition of short phrases.
5. Triple meters and the use of hemiola within.
6. Mixed meters.
7. Melodic ornamentation.
8. The exclamation "Ay!" at the beginning or end of the song.

uncomplicated: see **accessible**.

varied: Containing many diverse melodic, harmonic, rhythmic, or textural configurations.

THE WORKS

1 Acuña, Luis Gustavo. *Ayer, Yo Fuí Feliz* (Spanish). c1990 Margaux em 5101. Text by composer. Medium B3-F5/B3-F5. *M*. Utilizes musical idioms most often associated with traditional Spanish vocal music. Melodically repetitive, with long descending stepwise phrases balanced by leaps of M6 or more. Rhythms are quite accessible. Varied yet uncomplicated guitar accompaniment.

2 Adams, David. *Lunar Aspects* (English). 1996 composer. Text by various 10th- and 11th-century Japanese composers. Soprano C4-C6/D4-G#5. *VD*. Cycle of four songs (7'). Ethereal poems about the moon in diverse musical settings. Atonal, with many long, legato chromatic vocal phrases of varied melodic motion; leaps of sevenths and ninths are not uncommon. Intricate rhythms and some unusual meters. Guitar is challenging and prominent.

3 Adams, David. *Two Songs* (English). 1977/c1977 composer, also Australia Q783.66542/ADA1. Text by e. e. cummings from *selected poems, 1923-1958*. Soprano Bb3-B5/Ab4-Ab5. *VD*. Group of two songs (8'). Frequently dissonant, using serial composition techniques. Uncommon chromatic intervals are regularly employed. Changing meter sections combined with ametrical passages. Guitar utilizes unusual sounds such as "fluttered" notes and dragging fingernail on strings.

4 **Adler,** Samuel. *Ask Me* (English). c1991 Southern V-84. Text by various authors. Medium F3-A♭5/A3-E5. *D.* Cycle of four songs (12'). Tonal with wide, chromatic melodic leaps. Rhythms are challenging due largely to the numerous meter changes. A wide variety of moods is displayed. Difficult guitar part contains some very rapid passages.

5 **Alemann,** Eduardo Armando. *Pompas Fúnebres* (Spanish). 1974/c1981 Ricordi S.A. BA13294. Text by Antonio Espina. Soprano G3-B5/B3-G5. *VD.* Described as a cantata, the work consists of eight movements (15'). Atonal with disjunct, fragmented melodic motion. Widely varying tempi. Use of nontraditional techniques for both players such as sprechstimme, glissando, tamburo, and quarter tones.

6 **Almeida,** Laurindo. *Caboclo Brasil* (Portuguese). Brazilliance BP 528. Text by Junquilho Lourival. High B3-G#5/E4-E5. *M.* Diatonic with mixed melodic motion consisting of repeated short phrases, several of which encompass more than an octave. Simple rhythms in a light-hearted moderato tempo. English singing version provided. Very accessible, often chordal guitar accompaniment.

7 **Almeida,** Laurindo. *Caçador* (Portuguese). c1966 Brazilliance BP 200. Text by composer. Medium A3-C5/D4-B4. *E.* Mostly diatonic with repetitious, highly accessible melodic and rhythmic patterns. Guitar part is strictly accompanimental in nature, consisting of repeated chordal figures.

8 **Almeida,** Laurindo. *Choro e Batuque* (Portuguese). c1962 Brazilliance BP 201. Text by composer. High G3-A5/E4-F#5. *D.* Mostly diatonic. Contains numerous melismas, some with fairly wide (P5 or larger) intervals. Varied rhythms include much syncopation. Sustained forte A5. Middle section calls for nonpitched rhythmic sounds and humming. Active guitar accompaniment is not difficult.

9 **Alvarez,** Luis Manuel. *Alvarada Boricuo-Cubana* (Spanish). 1982/c1986 Puerto Rico. Text by Nicolas Guillén. Medium C4-E5/C4-A4. *M.* From the collection *La Canción de Arte en Puerto Rico.* Mostly diatonic, with a notable Spanish flavor in 8/16 meter. Very rhythmic, disjunct vocal line, with a predominance of m3 and M3 intervals. Guitar part primarily consists of repeated arpeggio-like accompaniment patterns.

10 **Alvira,** José Rodriguez. *Dos Canciones* (Spanish). 1975/c1986 Puerto Rico. Text by Juan Antonio Corretjer. High D4-F5/D4-F5. *M.* Group of two songs (6') from the collection *La Canción de Arte en Puerto Rico.* Many meter changes from 2/4 to 6/8 in first song. Effective contrast between the songs in terms of melodic contour, tessitura, rhythms, and accompaniment. Varied but uncomplicated guitar part.

11 Angelis, Ugalberto de. *Tre Canti* (Italian). 1967/c1974 Sonzogno 2901. Text by Giorgio Vigolo. High C4-A5/F♯4-F♯5. *VD*. Group of three songs (7'15"). Atonal, with frequent meter changes. Very disjunct melody in first song, featuring unusual chromatic intervals. Complex rhythms in all three songs. Highly demanding guitar part requires many harmonic and percussive sound effects.

12 Apivor, Denis. *Seis Canciones* (Spanish). 1945/c1972 Berben E. 1640 B. Text by Federico García Lorca. High B3-A♭5/E4-E5. *D*. Group of six songs (23') of noticeable Spanish character. Most songs feature melodic ornamentations typical of that style. Meter and tempo changes not uncommon. Utilizes many moods, including powerful, dramatic sections. Challenging, substantial guitar.

13 Argento, Dominick. *Letters from Composers* (English). c1971 Boosey BH BK 686. Text from famous composers' letters. High A3-A5/E4-G5. *D*. Group of seven songs (20'). Mainly tonal, with frequent chromaticism. Much stylistic contrast between songs, as each often utilizes the musical manner associated with the featured composer. Some songs contain humorous text. Challenging and substantial guitar part.

14 Armstrong, John G. *An die Musik II* (English). 1985/c1985 Canada MV 1102 A736an. Text by various authors. Soprano B3-A5/D4-F5. *D*. Cycle of five songs (15'). Much chromaticism with smooth melodic motion. Contrasting moods within cycle. Humorous text in third song (*An die Musik*), and the first and last are retrograde (text and pitches) to each other, with words by Shakespeare.

15 Arseneault, Raynald. *Ave Maria* (Latin). 1991/c1991 Canada MV 1102 A781av. Text from Roman Catholic liturgy. Soprano A♭3-C5/C4-G5. *D*. Atonal and ametrical. Some unusual chromatic intervals, but generally a smooth melodic approach. A wide array of dynamics is required throughout entire pitch range. Guitar part consists mostly of isolated tones with harmonics, usually in unison with the voice.

16 Aschero, Sergio. *España Canto y Poesia* (Spanish). c1973 Alpuerto ALP 19736. Text by Federico García Lorca. Various ranges G3-G5/G3-G5. *E*. Collection of songs and song groups for voice(s) and guitar in a variety of pitch ranges and moods. All of the music features simple melodies with elementary guitar accompaniments.

17 Asriel, Andre. *Jiddische Volkslieder (Berufs- und Ständelieder)* (Yiddish). c1978 Neue NM 381. High or Medium B3-E5/E4-D5. *E*. Collection of 16 strophic work and social songs. One of three volumes of Yiddish folk songs arranged by Asriel (see other entries), with subtle, interesting accompaniments that are often mildly unconventional. Yiddish is transcribed phonetically;

German singing translation also provided. Accompaniment is written for piano. Alternate guitar accompaniment part available as NM 381a.

18 Asriel, Andre. *Jiddische Volkslieder (Kinder- und Wiegenlieder)* (Yiddish). c1981 Neue NM 416. High or Medium A3-E5/E4-D5. *E.* Collection of 16 strophic children's songs and lullabies. One of three volumes of Yiddish folk songs arranged by Asriel (see other entries), with subtle, interesting accompaniments that are often mildly unconventional. Yiddish is transcribed phonetically; German singing translation also provided. Accompaniment is written for piano. Alternate guitar accompaniment part available as NM 416a.

19 Asriel, Andre. *Jiddische Volkslieder (Liebeslieder)* (Yiddish). c1992 Neue NM 359. High or Medium B♭3-E5/E4-D5. *E.* Collection of 16 strophic love songs. One of three volumes of Yiddish folk songs arranged by Asriel (see other entries), with subtle, interesting accompaniments that are often mildly unconventional. Yiddish is transcribed phonetically; German singing translation also provided. Accompaniment is written for piano. Alternate guitar accompaniment part available as NM 359a.

20 Asriel, Andre. *Treue* (German). c1971 Neue NM 285. Text by Heinrich Heine. Medium A3-D5/D4-D5. *E.* From the 12-song collection … *und die Liebe braucht ein Dach*, compiled by Helge Jung and Werner Pauli. Simple, diatonic song in strophic form. Accessible, repetitive guitar accompaniment.

21 Azpiazu Iriarte, José de. *Cinco Canciones Populares Españolas* (Spanish). c1958 Union UMG19403. Text by various authors. High D4-A5/E4-E5. *M.* Group of five traditional Spanish folk songs (12'), with revised accompaniments. Few stylistic ornamentations required. Little change in musical mood from piece to piece. The guitar accompaniment differs in each song, yet is not difficult.

22 Azpiazu Iriarte, José de. *La Flor de la Canela* (Spanish). c1955 Symphonia Sy. 408. Text by composer. High B3-G5/E4-E5. *M.* Utilizes musical qualities associated with traditional Spanish folk songs. Most noteworthy and challenging are the numerous rapid, turn-like vocal ornamentations. Substantial, prominent guitar part.

23 Azpiazu Iriarte, José de. *Homenaje a Manuel de Falla* (Spanish). 1949/c1958 Union UMG19400. Text by composer. Medium C♯4-A4/C♯4-A4. *E.* Mostly diatonic. Features a lengthy but uncomplicated guitar introduction followed by a somewhat brief, simple vocal part which is then repeated.

24 Azpiazu Iriarte, José de. *Noche de San Juan* (Spanish). 1962/c1962 Union UMG19985. Text by J. Herrera Petere. High E4-A5/A4-F♯5. *M.* Noticeable traditional Spanish folk song characteristics. Several trills and other ornamentations required. Singer must diminuendo to pianissimo on sustained F#5 at end of piece. Simple guitar accompaniment, consisting mostly of chords.

25 Azpiazu Iriarte, José de. *Recuerdo* (Spanish). 1962/c1962 Union UMG19886. Text by J. Herrera Petere. High C4-G5/E4-E5. *M.* Utilizes many idioms of Spanish folk songs. Alternating measures of 6/8 and 3/4. Requires singer to glissando to a sustained E5, and then diminuendo. Varied guitar part, while not difficult, includes pizzicato and harmonics.

26 Azpiazu Iriarte, José de. *Zorongo Gitano* (Spanish). c1955 Symphonia Sy. 407. Text by composer. Medium A3-E5/E4-D5. *E.* Incorporates many elements of traditional Spanish folk song. Very animated tempo and mood. Active, challenging guitar part.

27 Babbitt, Milton. *Four Cavalier Settings* (English). 1991 Peters P67533. Text by various authors. Tenor B2-A4/D3-Ab4. *VD.* Group of four songs (12'). Atonal, with fragmented, highly disjunct, chromatic melodic motion that features many wide intervals. Very challenging rhythms involve diverse meters and intricate subdivisions. Constantly changing array of often extreme dynamics. Very demanding, fragmented guitar.

28 Bach, Erik. *Mattoidens Sånger* (Danish). 1970/c1974 Egtved MF 289. Text by Gustaf Fröding. Baritone A2-E4/C3-C4. *D.* Cycle of six songs (9'). Quite varied in degrees of chromaticism and dissonance used in each song, yet all feature largely conjunct melodic motion and uncomplicated rhythms. Sprechstimme and recitative are used. Challenging, prominent guitar part.

29 Bakke, Ruth. *Hør, Alle Som Tørster* (Norwegian). 1978 Norway S 400 BAK. Text from the Bible: *Isaiah* 56; *John* 6. Soprano Bb3-Gb5/F4-F5. *D.* Described as a motet, this atonal work features sustained, long, sometimes dramatic vocal phrases with mostly smooth melodic motion. Frequently changing meters produce challenging rhythms. Animated guitar part contains mostly eighth notes of single-note phrases or dissonant chords.

30 Balázs, Arpád. *Two Spanish Folksongs* (Spanish). c1996 Budapest Z. 14 101. High E4-F5/A4-E5. *E.* Group of two simple Spanish songs (2-5'), from the book *Playing on Six Strings. Easy Concert Pieces for Guitar.* Both songs are strophic, with the first containing 12 verses. Accessible yet active guitar parts can be optionally played as solo pieces.

31 Balfour, Ian. *Epigrams and Miniatures* (English). 1993 Scotland. Text by William Soutar. Bass Db2-Ab3/F2-F#3. *VD.* Cycle of eight short songs (8'). Atonal, with many uncommon chromatic intervals. Complex rhythms with unusual meters that change often. Challenging guitar part, sometimes written on two staves. The score calls for tenor, yet the range suggests a bass voice.

32 Barbosa-Lima, Carlos. *Three Argentine Popular Songs* (Spanish). c1991 *Guitar Review* #86. Text from *The Popular Song Book*. High D4-G5/E4-D5. *M*. Group of three traditional Argentine folk melodies (5') with revised, varied guitar accompaniments that utilize colorful harmonies and many harmonics. Generally slow tempi (M.M. 48-58). 6/8 and 3/4 interchange in first two songs. Some dramatic passages. English singing translation provided.

33 Bargielski, Zbigniew. *4 Piesni Milosne (4 Liebeslieder)* (Polish). 1969/c1975 composer, also Agencji PZCHO zam.141 n.250. Text by Alicja Patey-Grabowska from *Z kregu* and *Iskry*. Mezzo G3-A♭5/C4-E5. *VD*. Group of four songs (8'). Atonal and ametrical with very disjunct, long, chromatic vocal lines. Nontraditional notation includes blank measures, no rests, exclusive use of eighth notes, and stems with no pitch (no instructions given). Very sparse, chordal guitar is written on two staves due to its optional setting for piano. German singing translation provided.

34 Barnes, Milton. *Psalm 23* (English). 1973/c1973 Canada MV 1102 B261ps. Soprano E4-D5/F#4-C#5. *M*. Tonal with chromaticism, featuring long vocal phrases of mostly stepwise melodic motion with many repeated pitches and rhythms. Active, varied guitar accompaniment is not difficult.

35 Barnett, Carol Edith. *Voices* (English). 1983/c1983 composer. Text by Nancy Cox. Soprano B3-A5/D4-D5. *D*. Cycle of six songs (17'). Second song is for voice alone, and the fifth is for solo guitar. Chromatic, primarily stepwise melodic motion. Meter changes and some challenging rhythms. Contemporary text with feminist perspective, sometimes humorous.

36 Barth, Frode. *Den Onde Dronning* (Norwegian). 1992 Norway S 400 BAR. Text by Inger Hagerup. Mezzo D#4-E5/E4-E5. *E*. Tonal with some dissonant chromaticism. Short, simple ABA-coda structure. Varied melodic motion and repetitive dotted rhythms are quite accessible. Varied, animated guitar is somewhat more demanding than the voice part.

37 Barth, Frode. *Songen til Han Som er Komen Igjenom* (Norwegian). 1991 Norway S 400 BAR. Text by David Herbert Lawrence. Mezzo G#3-E5/C4-C5. *M*. Mostly diatonic with traditional harmonic progressions. Melodic motion is largely stepwise and consists of simple eighth- and quarter note rhythm patterns. Simple, often folk-like guitar patterns help provide a straightforward, uncomplicated musical impression.

38 Barton, Nicholas. *6 Animal Songs to God* (English). c1971 Andresier 0004. Text by children of St. Thomas. Mezzo A3-G5/D4-E5. *D*. Cycle of six songs (8'30"). Tonal with chromaticism, using widely varied melodic motion and rhythmic figures amidst many changes in meter and tempo. The texts are prayers to God by different animals, as written by children, and are often quite humorous. Diverse and prominent guitar part.

39 Bavicchi, John. *Three Songs* (English). 1984/c1985 BKJ. Text by Marilyn Lays Pinheiro. Soprano C4-A5/G4-E5. *D.* Group of three songs (10'). Tonally elusive with much chromaticism. Wide intervals are not uncommon, yet the melody maintains an overall smooth contour. Relatively fast, despite varying tempi, due to mostly eighth- and sixteenth-note rhythms in both voice and guitar.

40 Baxter, Garth. *A Cradle Song* (English). 1988/c1988 composer. Text by William Blake. Soprano C4-G5/E♭4-C#5. *M.* Tonal, with chromatic vocal lines that are long and somewhat disjunct, yet always supported harmonically by the accompaniment. Frequent simple meter changes. Rhythmically uncomplicated, as befitting the theme of the text. Active and equally important guitar part.

41 Baxter, Garth. *Grandmother, Think Not I Forget* (English). 1991/c1996 Creative. Text by composer. Soprano C4-G5/C4-E5. *M.* Mostly diatonic. Triplet eighth-note sections frequently alternate with sections of duple eighth notes. Many simple meter changes. Both voice and guitar require legato phrasing. Active, interesting guitar part is not complicated.

42 Baxter, Garth. *Three from Sara* (English). c1994 Columbia CO 345A. Text by Sara Teasdale. Soprano B3-E♭5/C4-D5. *M.* Group of three songs (9'). Volume 1 of the composer's series *From The Heart: Three American Women.* Tonal with accessible chromatic melodic motion. Diverse settings and tempi yield quite varied moods. Tessitura possibly better suited for a mezzo. Substantial and active guitar part.

43 Baxter, Garth. *Three Madrigals* (English). c1994 composer. High B3-F5/D4-D5. *M.* Group of three songs (10'). Reminiscent of Elizabethan madrigals through its use of melody and rhythm, yet with an accessible, contemporary harmonic scheme. Lightly textured, sometimes contrapuntal guitar configurations often suggest Renaissance-style lute accompaniment.

44 Baxter, Garth. *Two Remembrances* (English). c1994 Columbia CO 345B. Text by Susan Laura Lugo. Soprano B3-G5/C4-E♭5. *M.* Group of two songs (5'). Volume 2 of the composer's series *From The Heart: Three American Women.* Tonal with long, somewhat chromatic phrases of uncomplicated rhythms in slow tempi. Accessible, largely single-note guitar accompaniment helps to reinforce the work's simple, intimate nostalgia.

45 Baxter, Garth. *What Death Can Touch* (English). c1996 composer. Text by Chaim Stern. High D4-G5/G4-E5. *M.* Largely diatonic, with varied, uncomplicated melodic motion in a legato, relaxed setting (M.M. 72). Accessible rhythms are nonetheless diverse due to syncopations, triplets, and changing meters and tempi. Interesting guitar part is not difficult, and contributes to flowing feel within piece.

46 Baxter, Garth. *Willa* (English). c1994 Columbia CO 345C. Text by Willa Cather. Soprano C4-F#5/E4-D5. *D.* Cycle of four songs (12'). Volume 3 of the composer's series *From The Heart: Three American Women.* Tonally chromatic motion is sometimes challenging. Introspective texts; song #4 is about the American frontier, with Spanish-style guitar solos. Richly varied guitar part.

47 Beat, Janet. *Cat's Cradle for the Nemuri-Neko* (English). 1991/c1991 Bastet. Text by composer. Soprano or Mezzo G♭4-F5/A♭4-E♭5. *D.* Voice and guitar are in different tonalities, resulting in almost constant dissonances. Rhythmically uncomplicated with a relaxed, legato flow due to the guitar's steady single-note accompaniment. Requires purring and other feline sounds from singer.

48 Beat, Janet. *The Leaves of My Brain* (English). 1974 Bastet. Text by Mervyn Peake. High C4-A♭5/F4-F5. *D.* Atonal with disjunct melodic motion. Voice and guitar parts are somewhat fragmented. Humming required, along with short sections of vocalise. Piece is to be played in a somewhat rhythmically free, meditative manner. Mostly single-note phrases for guitar.

49 Beckwith, John. *Four Songs* (English). c1967 Canada MV 1102 B397fo. Text by Ben Jonson from *Volpone.* Baritone C3-E4/C3-E4. *M.* Group of four songs (5'). Diatonic with mostly stepwise melodic motion. Basic rhythm patterns are employed with changing meters. Simple guitar part, consisting of quarter- and half-note chords and brief passages of somewhat faster single-note accompaniment.

50 Behrend, Siegfried. *Fuenf Altjapanische Geishalieder* (Japanese). c1967 Sikorski 248. Text by various authors. Medium A3-F#5/D4-E5. *M.* Group of five songs (14') in romanized Japanese. Diatonic, lyric melodies with accessible rhythms in mostly strophic form. Some declamation required. Simple, primarily accompanimental guitar part.

51 Behrend, Siegfried. *Impressionen Einer Spanischen Reise* (Spanish). 1958/c1958 Sikorski H.S. 373f. High C4-F5/E4-F5. *M.* Suite of three traditional Spanish songs (10') with revised guitar accompaniments. First song requires rapid melodic ornamentations, while the third demands a powerful, declamatory vocal style. Challenging guitar part features many fast passages.

52 Behrend, Siegfried. *Suite nach Altpolnischen Melodien* (Polish). 1966/c1968 Bote bb 0944. High D4-F#5/F#4-E5. *M.* Suite of five songs based on old Polish melodies (5'). Diatonic with uncomplicated melodic motion and rhythms. Varies greatly in mood and tempo. Simple, repetitive guitar accompaniment.

53 Behrend, Siegfried. *Yo Lo Vi* (Spanish). 1959/c1971 Modern M 1608 E. Text by Francesco de Goya. High B♭3-E♭6/E4-B5. *VD.* Cycle of five songs

(10'). Often atonal, with uncomplicated rhythms. Each song varies greatly in terms of melodic difficulty; songs #1 and #4 are fairly simple, yet the others frequently use unusual intervals exceeding an octave, often in the extreme upper pitch range.

54 Bellocq, Ivan. *6 ChanteFables* (French). 1989 composer. Text by Robert Desnos from *ChanteFables*. High D4-Bb5/E4-E5. *M.* Group of six light-hearted songs (6'20") about animals. Tonal, with mostly stepwise chromatic melodic motion and simple, often fast rhythms in a variety of tempi. Much repetition due to repeated stanzas throughout. Song #4 has chromatic ascent to a sustained Bb5. Uncomplicated, active guitar is often texturally sparse.

55 Bellucci, Giacomo. *Canti Erotici* (Italian). 1987/c1989 Berben E. 3048 B. Text from *Canti Erotici dei Primitivi dell'Oceania*. Soprano or Mezzo C#4-Ab5/D4-E5. *D.* Atonal and fragmented, via many brief, markedly contrasting sections noted by aspects such as ametrical a cappella, percussive guitar, speaking, quasi-recitative, and various recurring guitar motives. Occasional wide leaps, including several D4-E5 glissandi. Varied and active guitar part.

56 Benedict, Robert C. *Alleluia (in a Neo-Baroque Style)* (English). c1982 Waterloo. Text by composer. Soprano B3-F#5/E4-C#5. *M.* Tonal and mostly diatonic, beginning with a simple melody in three verses of sacred text. Concludes with many short, accessible melismas on the word "Alleluia." Accompaniment is contrapuntal yet not complicated, and may be played on piano (a separate, somewhat different part is supplied).

57 Bentzon, Niels Viggo. *Song Cycle* (Danish). 1986 Hansen. Text by composer. Soprano E4-B5/G4-G5. *D.* Cycle of seven songs (18'). Chromatic with some dissonance, yet often tonal in concept. Requires rhythmic precision, but is not excessively demanding. No tempo indications are given. Guitar part contains mostly single-note phrases, and sometimes appears in bass clef.

58 Beraldo, Primo. *Intorno ad una Fonte* (Italian). c1982 Zanibon G. 5964 Z. Text by Giovanni Boccaccio. Medium E4-F#5/G4-E5. *D.* Tonal with chromaticism. Mostly stepwise melodic motion. Frequent meter changes, yet rhythms are not difficult. Legato lines interspersed with declamatory phrases. Brief sections of speaking and sprechstimme. Guitar part calls for numerous tone colors.

59 Berkeley, Lennox. *Songs of the Half-Light* (English). 1964/c1966 Chester JWC 4066. Text by Walter de la Mare. High D4-A5/G4-G5. *D.* Cycle of five songs (13'). Tonal with chromaticism. Meter changes are common, yet rhythmically uncomplicated. Songs vary greatly in terms of tempo and mood. Substantial, challenging guitar part.

60 Bettinelli, Bruno. *Due Liriche* (Italian). 1977/c1977 Zanibon G. 5669 Z. Text by composer. High E♭4-G5/G4-E5. *D.* Group of two songs (5'). First song is somewhat chromatic and lyrical, with frequent meter changes from 4/4 to 5/4. Second song is more chant-like, with numerous repeated pitches. Guitar part features several very rapid passages.

61 Biberian, Gilbert E. *And for the Soul* (English). 1967/c1967 composer. Text by George Seferis. Medium D4-E5/F#4-C#5. *M.* Short song (50"), utilizing chromatic melodic motion with simple rhythms. Slow, sustained and contemplative in nature. Accessible guitar part is largely chordal and accompanimental in design.

62 Biberian, Gilbert E. *Cantos Nuevos* (Spanish). 1966/c1975 composer. Text by Federico García Lorca. Tenor C#3-C5/E3-A4. *D.* Group of eight songs (25'). Atonal with much dissonance. Mostly stepwise melodic motion using intricate and varied rhythms. Tessitura of fourth song is very high. Several songs are spoken; they may be rendered by a separate reciter. Substantial, challenging guitar.

63 Biberian, Gilbert E. *Epigrams* (French). c1976 Berben E. 2079 B. Text by Jacques de Cailly. High E♭4-C6/F4-F#5. *D.* Cycle of four songs (8'). Largely disjunct vocal line, frequently dissonant against guitar. Rhythmically uncomplicated. One of several sustained, forte C6 appears at the very beginning of the cycle. Widely varied tempi and mood. Challenging guitar part.

64 Biberian, Gilbert E. *The Sick Rose* (English). 1967/c1967 composer. Text by William Blake. High G#4-G5/B4-F#5. *M.* Very short song (30") in an atonal setting with legato, mostly stepwise melodic motion. Triplet eighth notes in voice over sixteenth notes in guitar are common. Guitar part consists solely of a constantly repeated sixteenth-note accompanimental pattern.

65 Biberian, Gilbert E. *Upon Julia's Clothes* (English). 1966/c1966 composer. Text by Robert Herrick. High A4-G5/B4-G5. *M.* Very short song (30") in a tonal setting with varied yet simple melodic motion. Light, joyful mood, mostly in 6/8. Rhythms are quite accessible, even in several 7/8 and 5/8 measures. Active guitar part is largely chordal in configuration.

66 Bielawa, Herbert. *Emily Dickinson* (English). 1973 composer. Text by James Schevill. Tenor A2-G4/D3-D4. *D.* Tonal with much chromaticism. Sections of smooth melodic motion alternate with those featuring more disjunct motion in ametrical setting. Interpretive instructions given throughout for singer. Guitar part, consisting mostly of single-note phrases, has a solo interlude.

67 Bielawa, Herbert. *Miniatures* (English). 1984 composer. Text by Tony Thomas. High D4-G#5/E4-E5. *M.* Group of four songs (10'). Much chromaticism, with frequent long, legato lines. The first three songs have a somewhat relaxed mood, while the fourth is more animated and rhythmically exacting. Guitar part calls for "spider-like" finger motion in different parts of the second song.

68 Binnie, James. *Landscapes* (English). 1970 Scotland. Text by Thomas Stearns Eliot. Tenor C3-G#4/E3-E4. *D*. Group of five songs (18') about various geographical locations. Tonally elusive, with much chromaticism. Considerable variety in terms of melodic motion, rhythm, tempo, and mood between each piece. Active, challenging guitar part.

69 Bjerno, Erling D. *Delfinen* (Danish). 1976/c1976 composer. Text by Thorkild Bjørnvig. Mezzo B3-F5/E4-B4. *D*. Cycle of three songs (7'). Vocal line consists of mostly repeated notes with complex ametrical rhythmic divisions, yielding a recitative-like style. Guitar part features similarly complex, yet contrasting patterns, thereby making rhythmic precision somewhat challenging.

70 Bjerno, Erling D. *Hans Christian* (Danish). 1976/c1977 Egtved MF 324. Text by Hans Christian Andersen. Medium A3-D5/C4-C5. *M*. Group of 21 songs (35'). Diatonic with simple rhythms. With the exception of two recitative selections, all songs are strophic, many of which contain five or six verses. Guitar part consists of straightforward repeated patterns which differ in each song.

71 Bjerno, Erling D. *Tidernes Følge* (Danish). 1975/c1975 composer. Text by Til Torben. Bass G2-C#4/C3-C4. *D*. Cycle of seven songs (17'). Features numerous groupings of repeated pitches in various rhythms which are often ametrical, yielding a recitative-like quality. Texturally sparse, repetitious guitar part is occasionally demanding in terms of changing, unusual rhythmic subdivisions.

72 Bland, William. *Four Songs* (English). 1973/c1973 composer. Text by Laurence Glass. Soprano Eb4-Bb5/F4-G5. *VD*. Group of four songs (10'). Chromatic, disjunct vocal lines that employ speaking, whispering, and quarter tones. Singer must rub knives together in last song. Guitar part calls for a "snare drum" effect. Utilizes nontraditional notation, especially in the second song (for solo guitar).

73 Bland, William. *2 Songs* (English). 1985 composer. Text by Rick Myers. Mezzo G3-E5/D4-D5. *VD*. Group of two songs (9'). Highly chromatic, with microtones and complex meters and rhythms. There are also unmetered sections, some of which do not require synchronization between voice and guitar. Voice part is mostly disjunct, yet legato. Requires use of bottleneck for guitar.

74 Bland, William. *Song* (English). 1977 composer. Text by Rick Myers from *Is*. Soprano D4-G5/F4-F#5. *VD*. Chromatic, with use of quarter tones.

Ametrical, and includes complex rhythmic divisions. Contains sections where voice and guitar need not coordinate rhythmically. Long, legato vocal lines. Highly challenging and varied guitar part.

75 Blomdahl, Karl-Birger. *Lugete, O Veneres Cupidinesque* (Latin). 1949 Sweden T-1143. Tenor F3-A♭4/F3-G♭4. *D.* Atonal, with various slow tempi, yielding overall tranquil mood. Long, mostly smooth chromatic vocal lines. Ametrical with uncomplicated rhythms. Guitar part generally features sparsely played, dissonant chords in recitative-like sections or simple, relaxed sixteenth-note phrases.

76 Blumenfeld, Harold. *Rilke* (German). 1975/c1977 MMB X815003. Text by Rainer Maria Rilke. Medium F#3-A#5/A3-F5. *VD.* Cycle of three songs (5"). Atonal, with many complex rhythms and frequent wide melodic leaps often exceeding an octave. Requires a wide dynamic range. Whispering is utilized in second song. Demanding, prominent guitar part.

77 Bochmann, Christopher. *Complainte de la Luna en Province* (French). 1974 composer. Text by Jules Laforgne. Tenor C3-C#5/D#3-E4. *VD.* Atonal, with highly disjunct, chromatic melodic motion in broken phrases. Frequent changes of unusual meters, such as 5/24, and complex rhythmic divisions within. Calls for wide dynamic range that varies often and abruptly. Requires soft falsetto C#5 at end. Challenging, fragmented guitar part.

78 Bondon, Jacques. *Trois Complaintes* (French). 1983/c1984 Eschig ME 8528. Text by Yvon Mauffret. Soprano E4-G5/G4-E5. *M.* Group of three songs (8'). Tonal with chromaticism, featuring accessible melodies in a light-hearted vein. Several meter changes, yet rhythms are straightforward. Guitar part varies from piece to piece, and is essentially accompanimental in nature.

79 **Bonneau,** Gilles Yves. *Permets-toi les jours heureux* (French). 1968 composer. Bass C3-C4/D3-G3. *E.* Diatonic melody consisting mostly of repeated pitches on various scale steps with simple eighth- and sixteenth-note rhythms in strophic form. Simple guitar part, comprised almost entirely of quarter- and eighth-note block triads.

80 Borup-Jørgensen, Axel. *Songs for Soprano and Guitar on Poems by Ole Sarvig* (Danish). 1985/c1985 Borup. Text by Ole Sarvig. Soprano A#3-G#5/C4-F5. *VD.* Group of 3 songs (12'). Atonal and mostly ametrical. Very fragmented due to numerous fermatas, yielding an ethereal ambience that centers on diverse tone colors and effects, such as tremolo, glissando, harmonics, and various plucking techniques, all in a relatively muted dynamic range.

81 Borup-Jørgensen, Axel. *3 Gammelkinesiske Digte* (Danish). 1983/c1983 Borup. Text by various 6th- and 8th-century Chinese poets. Mezzo G3-B4/B3-A♭4. *D.* Cycle of three songs (8'). Atonal, with ametricality implied from slow, long, legato phrases of varied rhythms and meters. Restrained dynamic range throughout. Second song is essentially a cappella. Dissonant guitar part is mostly chordal, and was originally written for lute.

82 Bosseur, Jean-Yves. *Trois Sonnets de Louise Labé* (French). 1987/c1987 composer. Text by Louise Labé. Medium F3-F#5/D4-E5. *VD.* Group of three songs (6'). Atonal, with chromatic melodic motion that combines wide, uncommon intervals and repeated pitches to produce notably angular vocal line. Challenging rhythms and changing meters. Relatively consistent mood and tempi throughout. Guitar is quite independent of the voice.

83 Böttcher, Eberhard. *Die Gläserne Brücke* (German). 1977 Norway S 400 BÖT. Text by Fritz Böttcher. Tenor D3-F#4/F#3-E4. *D.* Cycle of three strophic songs (8'). Atonal, with long legato phrases that are quasi-serialistic. Constant meter changes, yet rhythms are simple. No dynamics are indicated. Varied in tempo, yet little overall change in mood due to repetitious nature of both voice and guitar parts.

84 Bredemeyer, Reiner. *Ach, Es War Nur die Laterne* (German). 1972/c1975 Neue NM 315. Text by Julie Schrader. Medium F#3-G5/C4-E5. *M.* Cycle of 13 short songs (10'). Mostly diatonic melodies over a more chromatic accompaniment that is sometimes dissonant with the voice. Uncomplicated, repetitive rhythms yield a simple, direct quality. Some of the texts are light-hearted in nature. Sparse yet varied guitar.

85 Bredemeyer, Reiner. *Dr. Martin Luther Macht Gesange* (German). 1981/c1983 Peters P13225. Heldensoprano A♭3-C♭5/C4-A4. *D.* Cycle of 13 short untitled songs (8'). Atonal, with chromatic, fragmented vocal phrases of narrow tessitura which frequently yield a recitative-like quality. Several songs have numerous meter changes. Active, challenging guitar part.

86 Bredemeyer, Reiner. *Drei Chamisso—Lieder* (German). 1987/c1994 Neue NM 2047. Medium or Low G3-B4/B♭3-B4. *M.* Cycle of three short songs (5'). Atonal, with angular, chromatic melodic motion and accessible rhythms. Songs #1 & 3 are strophic. Song #2 is very short (30") and repetitive within. Cynical allusions to topical subjects (i.e., DDR, Gorbachev, Chernobyl), expressively aided by dissonant, fragmented guitar. Also see entry #88.

87 Bredemeyer, Reiner. *13 Heine-Lieder* (German). c1976 Peters P12851. Text by Heinrich Heine. Various ranges G3-C#6/G3-G5. *D.* Collection of 13 songs for various voices, largely high and low. Includes optional parts for clarinet/saxophone, percussion and organ. Various songs utilize extreme tessitura, and some feature speaking. Very simple guitar part, with occasional chord symbols.

88 Bredemeyer, Reiner. *....wie immer* (German). 1987/c1994 Neue NM 2047. Text by O. Mandelstam. Tenor or Baritone B♭2-F#4/E♭3-D4. *M.* Cycle of three short songs (5'), printed with composer's *Drei Chamisso—Lieder* (see entry #86). Atonal, with varied yet accessible chromatic melodic motion and rhythms. Song #1 uses oft-repeated voice and guitar motives. Songs #2 & 3 are very short; the former is strophic. Each song is titled by dates in the 1930s of Russian significance.

89 Bresgen, Cesar. *Fünf Rumänische Gesänge* (Rumanian). c1970 Hansen. Text from Rumanian folk songs. Mezzo A3-D5/B3-B4. *E.* Group of five traditional Rumanian folk songs (10'), each of which is strophic in form. Guitar part is active and varied, but not excessively demanding. The mood and tempo change for each song.

90 Bresgen, Cesar. *Von Wäldern und Zigeunern* (German). 1981/c1983 Tonos 7260. Text by H.C. Artmann. Any voice range B3-C#5/E4-B4. *D.* Cycle of four songs (15'). The singer mostly speaks, with the words printed over the guitar music. The few sections specifying notes and/or rhythms are extremely brief and simple. The guitar part, being in the musical forefront, is highly challenging.

91 Bresgen, Cesar. *Zwei Lieder* (German). c1990 Doblinger GKM 169. Text by various authors. High A3-G#5/E4-E5. *M.* Group of two songs (5'). Tonal with chromaticism, yielding numerous dissonances. Rhythmically uncomplicated, with regular simple meter changes. Mostly disjunct melodic motion, utilizing intervals generally smaller than P4. Guitar part is substantial but not difficult.

92 Britten, Benjamin. *Folksong Arrangements, Vol. 6* (English). c1961 Boosey 18814. High C4-G5/G4-E5. *M.* Group of six songs (18'). Traditional British and American folk songs with updated, innovative guitar accompaniments. Widely varied in tempo and mood. Substantial, sometimes highly demanding guitar part. The other volumes (1-5) feature piano accompaniment.

93 Britten, Benjamin. *Songs from the Chinese* (English). 1957/c1959 Boosey 18505. Text from ancient Chinese poetry. High Eb4-A5/E4-F#5. *D.* Cycle of six songs (15'). Tonal with chromaticism. Some pieces have frequent meter changes, yet the rhythms are not too difficult. Aided by unusual texts, the music expresses a wide range of emotion. Guitar part is varied and challenging.

94 Bröder, Alois. *14 Haiku* (German). 1994 composer. Soprano Cb3-C6/C4-G5. *VD.* Group of 14 short songs (16'). Atonal, with a very wide pitch range (over three octaves). Several songs feature extremely fast melismas. Highly varied musical settings. Requires nontraditional sounds for both voice and guitar, such as sprechstimme, and glissandi of varying speeds.

95 Brojer, Robert. *Vier Lieder* (German). 1968/c1980 Bommer B 1 B. Text by Peter Rosegger. Medium C#4-E5/E4-D5. *E.* Group of four strophic songs (10'). Diatonic with simple rhythms. Well-balanced between stepwise and simple disjunct melodic motion. Guitar consists of uncomplicated, lightly textured accompanimental patterns.

96 Brouwer, Leo. *Dos Canciones* (Spanish). c1993 Doberman DO 141. Medium A♭3-F5/C4-C5. *M.* Group of two songs (5'). Tonal, featuring much disjunct melodic motion with several unusual chromatic intervals. Simple rhythms despite some meter changes. Texts are folk-like in their unpretentious simplicity. Significant tempo contrasts. Varied guitar part.

97 Brumby, Colin. *Three Songs* (English). 1981 Australia Q783.4542/ BRU 7. Text by various authors. Medium B3-F5/E4-D5. *M.* Group of three songs (10'). Largely diatonic melodies, with much smooth, conjunct melodic motion. Fast tempo in second song requires some agility and use of portamento. Varied in mood and tempo. Guitar part is not difficult, and accompanimental in nature.

98 Brustad, Karsten. *Molnkurvor* (Swedish). 1986 Norway S 400 BRU. Text by Sven-Eric Johanson. Soprano E4-A5/E4-A♭5. *D.* (7'30"). Atonal, based on serialistic vocal motive that is frequently repeated throughout the work. Long, legato vocal lines are often chromatic and disjunct. Contrasting, less active middle section utilizes reciting, wordless vocalise, and humming. Guitar often features ostinato-like phrases.

99 Brustad, Karsten. *To Hansum Dikt* (Norwegian). 1987 Norway S 400 BRU. Text by Knut Hamsun from *Det Ulde Kor og Andre Dikte.* Soprano B3-A5/B3-C♯5. *D.* Group of two atonal songs (8'10"), both featuring the same serialistic vocal motive. The main differences between the two lie in the vocal rhythms and repeated guitar patterns, neither of which are complicated. Long, legato yet disjunct vocal lines in both songs. Speaking and humming required.

100 Burdick, David. *Songs on Texts of Edgar Allan Poe* (English). 1986/c1996 Creative. Text by Edgar Allan Poe. Soprano C4-A5/E4-E5. *D.* Group of eight songs (18'). The last six (each untitled and relatively brief) are collectively named *The Happiest Day.* Tonal with much chromaticism, featuring varied melodic motion in legato phrases set to diverse tempi and moods. Active, prominent guitar has many solo passages.

101 Burgon, Geoffrey. *Lunar Beauty* (English). 1986/c1993 Chester CH 59519. Text by various authors. Tenor or Medium A2-A4/D3-E4. *D.* Cycle of six songs (12'). Tonal with some chromaticism, yielding mild dissonances (usually major seconds) in the guitar. Uncomplicated, often stepwise melodic motion. Slow to moderate tempi throughout with mostly simple rhythms despite meter changes. Active, complemental guitar part.

102 Butterworth, Neil. *I Saw a Jolly Hunter* (English). 1977 Scotland. Text by Charles Causley. Medium D4-E5/G4-D5. *E.* Diatonic, with largely smooth, stepwise melodic motion and repetitive, simple rhythm patterns. Light, humorous text supported by animated tempo and rhythms. Guitar part is not difficult, except for a few brief sixteenth-note passages.

103 Campolieti, Cecilia S. *Gabbiani* (Italian). 1982/c1990 Pizzicato P 131 E. Text by Vincenzo Cardarelli from *Lo Specchio*. Medium D4-E5/E4-C#5. *M*. Mostly disjunct melodic motion in a chromatic setting. Words are often set to speech-like rhythms. Frequent use of melodic and rhythmic motives, often shifting from voice to guitar. Guitar part is not complicated, yet is constantly varied.

104 Carfagna, Carlo. *Aipnos* (Italian). 1991/c1995 Berben E. 3828 B. Text by composer. Soprano C4-A5/Ab4-F#5. *D*. Atonal, with contrasting sections noted by changing tempi, ametricality, speaking, and diverse guitar motives and soli, providing a somewhat ethereal ambience. Vocal line is chromatic yet not disjunct; its pitches are often doubled in the guitar. Quite accessible rhythms for both players.

105 Carroll, Nancy. *When I Am Dying* (English). c1978 *Chelys* v.2 #3. Text by Lawrence Hope. Medium B3-C#5/B3-B4. *E*. Diatonic with simple melodic motion and rhythms consisting solely of quarter notes and half notes. Very accessible, largely single-note guitar accompaniment.

106 Casséus, Frantz. *Haitienesques* (French). c1969 Colombo FC 2751. Text by composer. Medium B3-G5/E4-E5. *M*. Group of four songs (10'). Contains many musical aspects that are of Caribbean influence, most noticeably in each parts' rhythmic repetition and structure. Some melismatic singing required. Both voice and guitar parts vary widely in mood and tempo.

107 Castelnuovo-Tedesco, Mario. *Ballata Dall'Esilio* (Italian). 1956/ c1979 Berben E. 2252 B. Text by Guido Cavalcanti. Medium A3-F5/D4-D5. *M*. Tonal with many long, lyric vocal phrases. Slow tempo and minor key help to give the piece a brooding, plaintive quality. Simple, repetitive rhythms throughout. Great contrasts in dynamics required. Guitar part is mostly chordal and accompanimental.

108 Castelnuovo-Tedesco, Mario. *The Divan of Moses Ibn-Ezra* (English). 1966/c1966 Berben E. 1713 B. Text by Moses-Ibn-Ezra. High B3-A5/E4-F5. *D*. Cycle of 19 songs (35'), divided into five parts and an epilogue, with songs in each section having a common textual theme. Mostly diatonic with conventional rhythms. Widely varied in musical styles and expression. Challenging guitar part. Also see entry #109.

109 Castelnuovo-Tedesco, Mario. *Der Diwan des Moses-Ibn-Ezra* (German). 1966/c1990 Berben E. 3276 B. Text by Moses-Ibn-Ezra. High B3-A5/ E4-F5. *D*. Cycle of 19 songs (35'). A reissue of the composer's *The Divan of*

Moses Ibn-Ezra with a German singing translation by Erich Jung. See entry #108.

110 Castelnuovo-Tedesco, Mario. *Platero y Yo* (Spanish). 1960/c1973 Berben E. 1701,2,3,4 B. Text by Juan Ramón Jiménez. Any voice range G#3-D5/G#3-D5. *D.* Cycle of 28 songs (110') for narrator and guitar. Two songs contain brief singing passages: *Ronsard* (#11) and *La Arrulladora* (#18). A narrative in English, chosen by the composer, is also provided. Varied, challenging guitar part is more prominent than the voice.

111 Castelnuovo-Tedesco, Mario. *Vogelweide* (German). 1958/c1987 Berben E. 2639 B. Text by W. von der Vogelweide. Baritone A2-G4/G3-F4. *D.* Cycle of 10 songs (30'). Uncomplicated, often repetitive melodies that, like the guitar part, are mostly diatonic. Requires a high baritone voice with a secure G4. Guitar part is largely chordal, yet features several contrasting, difficult sections.

112 Charlton, Richard. *Dust on a Butterfly's Wing* (English). 1993/c1993 composer, also Australia 783.66547/CHA 1. Text by Minnie Agnes Filson. Soprano C4-G5/D4-E5. *M.* Cycle of seven songs (20'). In composer's words, "songs of nature, time and infinitesimal things." Long, legato phrases of uncomplicated rhythms, and strongly tonal. Wide array of moods and musical expression. Varied guitar part is generally more difficult than the voice.

113 Chiti, Gian Paolo. *Wer Zum Ersten Male Liebt* (German). 1970 composer. Text by Heinrich Heine from *Die Heimkehr.* Soprano F4-Ab5/Ab4-F5. *D.* Atonal with stepwise, highly chromatic melodic motion in mostly eighth- and quarter-note rhythms. Frequent meter changes. Guitar part consists mostly of quarter- and half-note dyads or sixteenth-note patterns, and is often dissonant to the voice.

114 Chopard, Patrice. *Schneelied* (German). 1989/c1989 New York Public Library. Text by Sarah Kirsch. Medium G4-F#5/A4-D5. *D.* (10'). Atonal with chromaticism. Words presented in syllable fragments, often repeated several times over a limited set of pitches with varied rhythms. Some speaking required. Sparse guitar part, consisting mostly of single pitches and dyads.

115 Chopard, Patrice. *Tagwache* (German). 1985 New York Public Library. Text by Hans Hehlen from *Augenblicke aus dem Fenster.* Alto G3-A5/C#4-E5. *VD.* Atonal, with fragmented vocal phrases alternating between stagnant and disjunct melodic motion. Outer sections are unmetered and measured in seconds; the middle uses changing meters in a "swing" rhythm. Some nontraditional sounds are required for both players. Sparse, dissonant guitar part.

116 Christensen, Mogens. *Morgenhav* (Danish). 1986 composer. Text by Ole Sarvig. Soprano G3-A#5/D4-G5. *VD.* Atonal with highly disjunct, chromatic melodic motion. Numerous meter changes and somewhat intricate rhythms. Slow, ethereal *adagio e serene molto* setting, aided by long vocal lines and thinly textured guitar part, both never exceeding pianissimo. Speaking, whispering required at end.

117 Colding-Jørgensen, Henrik. *Image.* c1992 composer. Any voice range. *D.* Chance composition for any number of instrumentalists or singers. Score consists entirely of abstract symbols and signs. The performers must choose one, musically interpret it, then go to another and interpret the relations between the two; the process continues until completion is desired.

118 Colding-Jørgensen, Henrik. *2 Songs by Keats* (English). 1988 Samfundet. Text by John Keats. Soprano C4-A♭5/F4-A♭5. *VD.* Group of two songs (8'). Atonal, with much dissonance between voice and guitar. Very legato vocal lines due to frequent melismas and adagio tempi. Some difficult rhythms involving unusual groupings. Very active and challenging guitar part.

119 Constant, Franz. *Je l'Aurais Pu Dire* (French). 1984 Belgium 95.689. Text by René Lyr. Medium C4-G5/F4-E5. *M.* Mostly tonal, with mixed melodic motion (intervals rarely exceed M3). Legato vocal phrases of repetitive, simple rhythms (despite changing meters) combined with a largely chordal guitar accompaniment in an andante tempo yields a tranquil mood. Guitar is sometimes dissonant to the voice.

120 Constant, Franz. *Trois Mélodies* (French). 1990 Belgium 95.697. Text by Charles Moisse from *Prague voici mon âme.* Mezzo A3-G5/C4-E♭5. *D.* Group of three songs (10'). Tonally elusive, yet the melody is largely diatonic. Vocal lines are somewhat disjunct with simple, repetitive rhythm patterns, often imitating speech. Frequent simple meter changes. Mood varies largely through changing tempi and sometimes very demanding guitar parts.

121 Cooijmans, Paul. *De Afstand* (Dutch). 1992 composer. Text by composer. Soprano G#3-A5/B3-F#5. *VD.* (7'). Atonal, with disjunct melodic motion often consisting of wide chromatic intervals. Complex rhythms and frequent changes of uncommon meters. Nontraditional sounds (e.g., coughing) are used. Guitar part is highly detailed and challenging.

122 Cooijmans, Paul. *Intermezzo a 2 Voci* (English). 1993 composer. Text by William Shakespeare. Soprano A3-F#5/A3-E5. *M.* Diatonic with stepwise motion and simple, repetitive rhythms in a moderato tempo. Sparse guitar accompaniment, consisting almost entirely of single pitches, is lute-like in nature. Voice part calls for sustained A3 several times.

123 Cooijmans, Paul. *Ut!* (Dutch). 1994 composer. Text by composer. Mezzo A#3-D#5/C#4-B4. *D.* Chromatic with mostly stepwise melodic motion. Rhythmically varied but not excessively complex. Guitar part, essentially chordal in design, is not difficult.

124 Cope, David. *Five Songs for Soprano and Guitar* (English). c1976 Seesaw. Text by composer. Soprano D4-G#5/G4-E5. *M.* Group of five short, untitled songs (2'30"). Tonal with chromatic, yet accessible melodic motion. Frequent meter changes occur, but rhythms are not difficult. Predominantly andante tempo and tranquil mood throughout. Uncomplicated guitar part.

125 Cordero, Ernesto. *4 Works for Voice & Guitar* (Spanish). c1993 Chanterelle ECH 708. Text by various authors. High D4-G5/E4-E5. *M.* Collection of four songs with noticeable Spanish flavor. Accessible diatonic melodies with some syncopation. Fourth song incorporates ametrical melismatic sections. Each song differs in mood and tempo. The varied guitar part can be challenging at times.

126 Cordero, Ernesto. *Mis Primeros Versos* (Spanish). c1992 Opera OT 029. Text by various authors. High C4-G#5/G4-F#5. *M.* Collection of eight songs composed largely from 1967 to 1974. Mostly diatonic with stepwise melodic motion and uncomplicated rhythms. Many long, legato vocal lines. Tempi usually within andante to moderato range. Active, accessible guitar accompaniments.

127 Creaghan, Andrew. *Poems of Li Po* (English). 1977 composer. Text by Li Po. High C#4-A5/E4-E5. *D.* Cycle of five songs (13'). Cycle #1 in the composer's four-cycle *Songs from the Tang Dynasty* (see other entries). Tonal with mostly very accessible melodic motion and rhythms, in varied meters and tempi. Many very long, legato vocal lines, some rather high in pitch. Guitar is primarily accompanimental, consisting of numerous uncomplicated, conventional patterns.

128 Creaghan, Andrew. *Poems of Po Chu-i* (English). 1977 composer. Text by Po Chu-i. High B3-A5/E4-F#5. *D.* Cycle of five songs (15'). Cycle #3 in the composer's four-cycle *Songs from the Tang Dynasty* (see other entries). Tonal with frequently long vocal lines of varied chromatic melodic motion. Numerous meter changes do not yield difficult rhythms. Several consistently high passages. Active guitar part features colorful harmonies.

129 Creaghan, Andrew. *Poems of Tu Fu* (English). 1978 composer. Text by Tu Fu. High D♭4-A5/G4-G5. *D.* Cycle of five songs (12'). Cycle #2 in the composer's four-cycle *Songs from the Tang Dynasty* (see other entries). Tonal with long, generally legato vocal lines of accessible melodic motion. Varied tempi and moods. Several vocal passages lie consistently above the staff. Active, substantial guitar part.

130 Creaghan, Andrew. *Poems of Wang Wei* (English). 1977 composer. Text by Wang Wei. High or Medium C#4-G5/E4-F#5. *D.* Cycle of five songs (13'). Cycle #4 in the composer's four-cycle *Songs from the Tang Dynasty* (see other entries). Tonal with extended vocal lines of diverse chromatic melodic motion that are sometimes dissonant to the guitar. Varied in mood and tempo. Very active guitar accompaniment.

131 Crockett, Donald. *Occhi dell'Alma Mia* (Italian). 1977/c1982 MMB S815001. Text from late 16th-century Italian love poems. High A♭3-B♭5/F♯4-F5. *VD.* (9'). Mostly chromatic, disjunct melodic motion with many wide intervals in long, sustained phrases. Often dissonant and varied in mood. Wide dynamic range at all pitch levels. Ametrical passages are combined with sections of changing meter. Very rapid, difficult, and colorful guitar part which occasionally utilizes quarter tones.

132 Crossman, Allan. *La Fille du Pêcheur* (several languages). 1980/c1980 composer, also AMC. Text by various authors from *La Fille* and *Out of the Cradle*. High G3-C6/C4-G5. *VD.* (16'30"). "Scène dramatique," depicting the crossing over into madness of a young woman waiting in vain for her dead sailor husband. Alternates French and English text. Covers a wide array of emotion. Chromatic and dissonant with much disjunct melodic motion. A wide dynamic range is necessary.

133 Davies, Peter Maxwell. *Dark Angels* (English). 1973/c1977 Boosey 20296. Text by George Mackay Brown. Mezzo E♭3-B♭5/B♭3-F5. *VD.* Cycle of three songs (12'), with the second song for solo guitar. Atonal with much dissonance. Highly disjunct chromatic melodies with many very wide intervals. Quasi-metrical, but vocal rhythms not difficult. Dark, morbid text. Highly challenging guitar part.

134 Dehler, Wolfgang. *Fünf Kiesel im Bach* (German). c1971 Neue NM 285. Text by Rose Nyland. Medium E4-E5/E4-C5. *E.* From the 12-song collection *...und die Liebe braucht ein Dach*, compiled by Helge Jung and Werner Pauli. Diatonic song with repetitious dotted eighth- and sixteenth-note rhythms. Simple meter changes. Easy, mostly chordal guitar accompaniment.

135 Dembski, Stephen. *Adult Epigram* (English). 1977 composer. Text by Wallace Stevens. Soprano E4-A5/F4-G5. *D.* Atonal with mixed, chromatic melodic motion that is dissonant to the guitar. Long, lyric vocal lines with accessible rhythms at an andante tempo. Uncomplicated, frequently repetitive guitar part is largely accompanimental, especially in first half of song.

136 Desderi, Ettore. *Due Cacce Quattrocentesche* (Italian). c1957 Berben E. 1112 B. High D4-G♯5/F♯4-F♯5. *D.* Group of two songs (7'). Tonal with chromaticism and some dissonance. Largely conjunct melodic motion. Rhythms and often fragmented vocal lines yield a quasi-speech effect. Active, substantial guitar accompaniment is not too difficult.

137 Dessagnes, Marybel. *Douleur Capitale* (French). 1994 composer. Text by Paul Eluard from *Capitale de la Douleur*. Mezzo G3-G5/B♭3-F5. *VD.* Cycle of six songs (13'33"). Atonal with much disjunct chromatic melodic motion, often containing leaps wider than m6. Quite varied in terms of rhythm, tempo, and mood. Features such nontraditional techniques as glissando and speaking. Difficult, substantial guitar part.

138 Dessau, Paul. *Der Adler* (German). 1973/c1975 Bote bb 1237. Text by Bertolt Brecht. High or Medium D4-E♭5/D4-E♭5. *D.* From the composer's *Tierverse von Bertolt Brecht*, a collection of five songs about animals for prepared piano with guitar and cello ad libitum. *Der Adler* (The Eagle) is atonal, with long, disjunct chromatic vocal phrases set to varied degrees of metricality. Challenges in the guitar part are primarily rhythmic.

139 Dessau, Paul. *Fünf Lieder* (German). 1969/c1970 DVfM 9042. Text by Eva Strittmatter. Bass G2-D4/B2-B3. *M.* Group of five songs (10'). Diatonic, with conjunct melodic motion. Vocal phrases tend to be fragmented. Although for bass voice, the songs are written in treble clef, to be sung an octave lower than written. Guitar consists largely of single-note accompaniment.

140 Dessau, Paul. *Sieben Rosen* (German). c1971 Neue NM 285. Text by Bertolt Brecht. Medium G4-E5/G4-C5. *E.* From the 12-song collection *...und die Liebe braucht ein Dach*, compiled by Helge Jung and Werner Pauli. Simple, diatonic song in strophic form with coda. Changing meters from 2/4 to 2/8 are repetitious and easy to perform. Easy yet effective guitar part.

141 Dessau, Paul. *Vom Kind, das Sich Nicht Waschen* (German). c1971 Neue NM 285. Text by Bertolt Brecht. Medium E4-C5/E4-C5. *E.* From the 12-song collection *...und die Liebe braucht ein Dach*, compiled by Helge Jung and Werner Pauli. Strophic song with mostly eighth-note rhythms. Simple meter changes. Accessible guitar accompaniment consists of repeated patterns.

142 Diaz, Gary. *Life Is a Circus* (English). 1988/c1988 composer, also AMC M1624 D542 L7. Text by composer. Tenor D3-B4/E3-E4. *M.* Cycle of four songs (7"). Vocal part, written in tenor clef, is mostly stepwise and diatonic, with uncomplicated rhythms. Text is somewhat light-hearted and introspective. Guitar part largely features repeated arpeggio and chordal passages.

143 Diaz, Gary. *Looking Up* (English). 1990/c1990 composer, also AMC M1624 D542 L8. Text by composer. Medium D#4-E5/A4-D5. *E.* Set in a quasi-"pop" style, most notably in its song structure and use of repeated syncopated melodies and text. Guitar part features simple arpeggio and chordal figures which are stated throughout the song.

144 Diaz, Gary. *New York, New York* (English). 1993 composer. Text by composer. High G4-B♭5/D4-A♭5. *E.* Utilizes "pop" style in terms of melodic repetition, vocal pitch range, syncopation and song structure. Light-hearted text about present-day New York City, citing many renowned landmarks. Simple guitar accompaniment consists mostly of quarter-note chords.

145 Dodgson, Stephen. *Four Poems of John Clare* (English). 1962 composer. Text by John Clare. High C#4-A5/E4-F5. *D.* Group of four songs (11'). Tonal with chromaticism. Greatly varied in terms of melodic motion, rhythm, dynamics and tempo as befitting the wide range of musical moods, from serious to light-hearted. Guitar part is substantial and often challenging.

146 Dodgson, Stephen. *London Lyrics* (English). 1977/c1978 composer. Text by various authors. High B3-A♭5/E4-F5. *D.* Cycle of five songs (16'). Tonal with chromaticism. Long, legato vocal lines of varied melodic motion. Some challenging rhythms. Requires a wide range of dynamics, including powerful, sustained high notes. Challenging and varied guitar part.

147 Domeniconi, Carlo. *Five Derwish Songs* (English). 1993 Margaux em 5104. Text from troubador songs of the Middle Ages. Medium G#3-F#5/D4-D5. *D.* Group of five songs (15'). Often tonally elusive with many austere modal melodies and harmonies. Text reflects Middle Eastern outlook, and its mood is largely muted and somber. Uniformly moderate tempi throughout with uncomplicated rhythms. Accessible guitar is essentially accompanimental.

148 Donatoni, Franco. *Åse.* 1990/c1990 Zerboni S. 10025 Z. Soprano C4-C6/F4-A5. *VD.* (10'). Atonal and ametrical, with chromatic and highly disjunct guitar phrases that are fragmented and complex rhythmically. The voice part occurs only sparingly, first consisting mostly of isolated glissandi on phonetic sounds, and later, sustained tones on parts of the word "magnus."

149 Dorward, David. *Horati Carminum* (Latin). Scotland. Text by Horace. High E♭4-B5/G4-F#5. *D.* Cycle of five songs (15'). Chromatic, with somewhat fragmented vocal lines. Melodic motion varies, with some unusual intervals in disjunct passages. Rhythms are generally uncomplicated. Requires pianissimo high notes. Varied guitar part is not too difficult.

150 Drogoz, Philippe. *Sur les Routes de Fer* (French). 1987/c1993 Eschig ME 8801. Text by Pierre Reverdy from *Sur les Routes de Fer.* Any voice range. *D.* For reciter and guitar; there are no sung vocal lines. The poetry is notated on the score in blocks, to be recited between guitar phrases, which is atonal and mostly ametrical. Improvisational in design, with a generally sparse, fragmented texture.

151 Duarte, John W. *A Cradle Song* (English). c1951 *Guitar Review* #12. Text by Padraic Colum. High B3-G5/E4-D5. *E.* Diatonic with mostly legato, disjunct motion of intervals no larger than P4. Easy, repetitive rhythms. Guitar part consists of legato, primarily chordal accompaniment with several harmonics at beginning and end of piece.

152 Duarte, John W. *Five Quiet Songs* (English). 1968/c1971 Berben E. 1520 B. Text by various authors. High C4-G5/E4-F5. *M.* Group of five songs (12'). Tonal with some chromaticism, featuring mixed melodic motion. Quasi-speech style in second song, yet not rhythmically difficult. Varied moods and themes; the final song deals with Christianity. Guitar part is largely accompanimental. Also see entry #154.

153 Duarte, John W. *Friends and Lovers* (English). c1994 Columbia CO 319. Text by various authors. High A#3-G5/E4-E5. *D.* Cycle of five songs (12'). Tonal with chromaticism, featuring much disjunct melodic motion. Rhythms tend to be repetitive within each song and generally easy. Varied in mood and tempo. Texts deal with friendship and love; the last song is light-hearted and best sung by a woman.

154 Duarte, John W. *Fünf Stille Lieder* (German). 1968/c1991 Berben E. 3326 B. Text by various authors. High C4-G5/E4-F5. *M.* Group of five songs (12'). A reissue of the composer's *Five Quiet Songs* with a German singing translation by Erich Jung. See entry #152.

155 Duarte, John W. *Grown-Up* (English). c1955 *Guitar Review* #18. Text by Edna Millay. High D4-F#5/F#4-D5. *E.* Very brief (11 measures) diatonic song with mostly uncomplicated disjunct melodic motion and simple rhythms. Guitar part consists of quarter- and eighth-note chordal accompaniment.

156 Duarte, John W. *Hark, Hark, The Ark!* (English). 1987/c1993 Columbia CO 320. Text by Spike Milligan from *Milliganimals* and *Silly Verse for Kids.* High Bb3-F#5/E4-F5. *M.* Cycle of six short songs (10'). Mostly diatonic, with uncomplicated rhythms. Much contrast in tempi and musical settings, which is further heightened by the consistently light-hearted, very humorous texts. Simple yet effective guitar accompaniment.

157 Dvořák, Charles. *The Bones of the Greeks* (English). 1984/c1986 Orphée DTMO-3. Text by various authors from *Resistance, Exile, and Love.* Soprano A#3-A5/B3-G5. *D.* Cycle of three songs (15'); the second is for solo guitar. The chromatic, often disjunct melodies utilize Greek modes. Frequent dissonances between voice and guitar, and long passages requiring good breath control. Guitar has solo interludes and optional modal cadenza.

158 Eben, Petr. *Písne K Loutne* (several languages). 1951/c1979 Supraphon H 6300. Text by various authors. Medium A#3-D5/B3-D5. *E.* Collection of six songs in different languages which include Czech, English, French and German. Diatonic with simple melodies and easy quarter- and eighth-note rhythms. Guitar part consists mostly of straightforward chordal accompaniment.

159 Egilsson, Arni. *Lullaby* (Spanish). 1993/c1993 Arnaeus, also Iceland ITM 068-025. Text by Federico García Lorca. Mezzo or Alto A3-C5/A3-C5. *E.* From the theatrical play *Bloodwedding.* Very simple, tranquil melody, befitting the mood implied by the work's title. Guitar part is quite accessible, consisting solely of repeated chords—one per measure—frequently found in popular music; guitarist is instructed to play *ad lib.*

160 Ehrström, Otto. *Fyra Visor för Sång och Gitarr* (Finnish). c1967 Fazer F.M. 4697. Text by various authors. High C4-G5/E4-E5. *M.* Group of four songs (4'). Mostly diatonic with simple, repetitive rhythms and varied yet accessible melodic motion. Uncomplicated guitar part consists largely of elementary chords and arpeggios.

161 Einem, Gottfried von. *Leib- und Seelen-Songs* (German). 1978/c1980 Bote bb 1357. Text by Lotte Ingrisch. High B3-A5/E4-E5. *M.* Group of five songs (12'). Largely diatonic with numerous large melodic leaps, some exceeding an octave. Varied musical settings yield widely contrasting moods between each song. Guitar part is not difficult, featuring mostly single-note accompaniments.

162 Einem, Gottfried von. *Liderliche Lieder* (German). 1982/c1983 Universal UE 17840. Text by Lotte Ingrisch. Medium C#4-E5/E4-C5. *D.* Cycle of three songs (12'). Mostly diatonic, but with some difficult chromatic sections. Largely conjunct motion due to many passages of repeated pitch. Changing meters, but rhythmically not complex. The text's theme centers around deviant sexual behavior.

163 Elias, Pedro. *Siete Canciones Sefardies* (Spanish). c1985 Union 22387. Medium B3-F#5/D4-D5. *M.* Group of seven songs (20'). Diatonic melodies with a strong Spanish flavor. First song has frequent unusual meter changes, but all other songs are rhythmically simple. Some fast melismas. Guitar part consists of mostly single-note accompaniment.

164 Ellis, Mark. *Rosenberg Sketches* (English). 1986/c1986 Andresier 0010. Text by Isaac Rosenberg. Baritone B2-F4/C3-D4. *D.* Cycle of four songs (10'). Tonal with frequent chromatic melodic motion and dissonances. Musically expressive settings of text dealing with World War I; varies greatly in terms of tempo, rhythm, and dynamics. Prominent and demanding guitar part.

165 Ellis, Mark. *Two Rilke Songs* (German). c1988 Andresier 0012. Text by Rainer Maria Rilke. Medium B3-E5/D4-D5. *M.* Group of two songs (5'). Diatonic with mostly stepwise melodic motion and uncomplicated rhythms. Both songs feature many long, connected vocal phrases in moderato tempi. Expressive use of dynamics. Active, repetitive guitar part is accessible and primarily accompanimental.

166 Enrichi, Arminio. *Quatre Chansons* (French). 1962/c1967 Zanibon G. 4895 Z. Text by various authors. Soprano D4-B5/F4-G5. *VD*. Group of four songs (10'). Each song differs greatly in its degree of tonality and quality of melodic motion. The first three songs feature long, legato lines. The fourth is more declamatory, and has opposing meters for voice (2/4) and guitar (3/4).

167 Erbse, Heimo. *Nachklänge* (German). 1973/c1975 Breitkopf BG 1082. Text by Joseph von Eichendorff. High E♭4-A♭5/F4-F5. *D*. Cycle of five songs (10'). Atonal with much dissonance, yet guitar often lends pitch support to the voice. Mostly conjunct melodic motion. Many long, legato lines. Extreme tempi (e.g., lento, vivace) are used. Rhythmically challenging, especially for guitarist.

168 Eyser, Eberhard. *Fredspris åt Herr Kissinger* (Swedish). 1973/c1973 Sweden T-1584. Text by Axel Strindberg. Mezzo D4-E♭5/E4-D5. *D*. Cycle of two songs (5'). Atonal and ametrical, with fairly smooth chromatic melodic motion of indefinite rhythms. Improvisational (instructions provided), with the option of adding one to three additional instruments and substituting piano for guitar.

169 Ezaki, Kenjiro. *Contention*. Casa 1004. Female C4-B5/F4-A5. *VD*. Aleatoric, atonal and nonrhythmic. Highly disjunct melodic intervals sung to phonetic sounds. Many nontraditional sounds such as shouting, roaring, laughing and breathy voice, along with sound effects on the guitar using the palm, fist, and plastics.

170 Farkas, Ferenc. *Cinque Canzoni dei Trovatori* (French). c1971 Berben E. 1512 B. Medium C♯4-E5/D4-E5. *M*. Cycle of five songs (7'). Modal, with predominantly stepwise motion. Easy rhythms, except for second song which contains several rapid melismas and ornaments. Guitar accompaniment is simple but varied.

171 Farkas, Ferenc. *Estampas Españolas* (Spanish). 1988/c1989 Berben E. 2999 B. Text by various authors. High C♯4-G5/E4-F5. *D*. Group of four songs (9'). Tonally elusive, via consonant harmonies functioning unconventionally. Somewhat chromatic melodies contain few sustained notes or phrases, and have varied yet not complex melodic motion and rhythms. Songs #1-3 feature relatively slow tempi. Song #4 is allegro vivace.

172 Farkas, Ferenc. *Gitárdalok* (Hungarian). 1983/c1985 Budapest 12897. Text by Jenó Dsida. Soprano E4-A5/F♯4-E5. *D*. Group of three songs (8'). Mostly diatonic with a strong sense of modality. Some dissonances and challenging rhythms. Requires strong A5. Guitar part is varied and somewhat challenging, and often works independently from the vocal melody.

173 Farquhar, David. *Blues and Pinks* (English). 1995/c1995 composer. Text by various authors. High C4-F#5/E4-E5. *M.* Group of five songs (13'). Tonal and always light-hearted in mood. Simple, repetitive melodic and rhythmic configurations in the voice and guitar accompaniment lend the music a quasi-"pop" feel.

174 Farquhar, David. *Swan Songs* (English). 1983/c1983 composer. Text by various authors. Medium A3-F#5/D4-D5. *D.* Cycle of seven short songs (13'). Tonal with some chromaticism. Several songs feature contrasting rhythms between voice and guitar (e.g., duple vs. triple). Some speaking and portamenti required. Varied guitar part is not excessively challenging.

175 Fink, Michael. *As My Heart Was* (English). c1983 Southern ST-400. Text by Robert Louis Stevenson. Baritone B2-E4/B2-B3. *M.* Cycle of five songs (8"). Primarily diatonic with accessible melodic motion and few difficult rhythms. Fourth song features many guitar harmonics.

176 Fink, Michael. *Three Devotional Miniatures* (English). c1992 Southern V-91. Text from biblical psalms. Soprano C4-A5/E4-E5. *M.* Group of three sacred songs (7'). Diatonic, with uncomplicated rhythms despite numerous simple meter changes. Energetic and consistently uplifting in spirit. Varied and active guitar accompaniment is not excessively challenging.

177 Fink, Siegfried. *Tangents CSB.* c1976 Zimmermann ZM 1970. Any voice range. *D.* Chance composition. Nontraditional score is written on a graph. Singer and guitarist primarily produce sounds which are not usually associated with music performances.

178 Finnissy, Michael. *Two Motets* (Latin). 1991 Oxford. Text by various authors. Countertenor G3-F5/B3-D5. *D.* Group of two songs (8'). Modal, chant-like melodies. Rhythmically intricate in both songs, but the first should be sung with molto rubato. Great contrast in tempo and mood between the two pieces. Challenging guitar part, requiring accompanimental flexibility.

179 Fitzgerald, Jonathan. *Songs from Omar Khayyam* (English). c1985 composer, also Australia 783.66542/FIT 1. Text by Omar Khayyam from *The Rubáiyát of Omar Khayyam.* Soprano C4-G5/E4-E5. *M.* Cycle of five songs (12'). Mostly diatonic, with stepwise melodic motion and uncomplicated rhythms. Simple guitar part, featuring primarily ostinato-like accompanimental configurations.

180 Förare, Erik. *5 Ironiska Sånger* (Swedish). 1986 Sweden A-300. Text by composer. Soprano Bb3-C6/E4-G5. *VD.* Group of five songs (22'). Atonal, with much disjunct melodic motion. Very complex rhythms and varied, highly detailed dynamic markings. Numerous playing instructions for guitar, which is written on two staves and is extremely challenging.

181 Ford, Clifford. *Halifax, 6 December 1917* (English). 1979/c1979 Canada MV 1102 F699ha. Text by composer. High C4-A5/G4-F5. *D.* Cycle of five songs (13'). Primarily diatonic with conjunct melodic motion. Most passages are not rhythmically complicated. Text deals with a historical disaster, and requires a great deal of expressiveness. Guitar part varies greatly in difficulty.

182 Forrester, Sheila Mary. *Three Songs for Countertenor* (English). 1993/c1994 composer. Text by Thomas Campion from *Two Bookes of Aires.* Alto or Countertenor G3-F5/D4-D5. *D.* Group of three songs (8'). Tonal, neo-Baroque style with the first and third song featuring more diatonicism and stepwise melodic motion. Uncomplicated rhythms despite frequent meter changes. Long, lyric vocal phrases, with unaccompanied melisma in song #3.

183 Fox, Christopher. *Whitman—Jefferies—Thoreau* (English). 1983/ c1987 English 2005 T. Text by various authors. Soprano C#4-C6/E♭4-A5. *VD.* Cycle of three songs (19'). Song #1 features isolated voice and guitar pitches sounded once every 5-15 seconds. Song #2 is minimalistic; the voice sings very long, gradually rising notes as the guitar becomes increasingly dense. Song #3 is atonal and utilizes many diverse musical settings.

184 Françaix, Jean. *Prière du Soir & Chanson* (French). c1950 Schott ED 4189. Text by various authors. High C4-B♭5/F4-F#5. *M.* Group of two songs (5'). Tonal, with colorful harmonies often used by 20th-century French composers such as Poulenc. Song #1 is subdued, featuring long, legato melodies over sustained guitar chords. Song #2 is quite animated and cheerful, with bouncy vocal lines and very rapid guitar.

185 Franco, Johan. *Ariel's Four Songs* (English). 1972/c1972 ACA 10924. Text by William Shakespeare from *The Tempest.* High D4-G5/F4-F5. *D.* Cycle of four songs (6'). Tonal with much chromaticism. The first song features frequent changes, yet overall rhythms are not too challenging. Three of the songs require loud, sustained high notes. Guitar part plays numerous single-note passages.

186 Franco, Johan. *Little Lamb* (English). 1977/c1977 ACA 13384. Text by William Blake. Medium F4-D5/F4-D5. *E.* Primarily diatonic with accessible chromaticism and simple rhythms at a slow tempo. Mostly stepwise motion, with melodic leaps no larger than P4. Text has religious overtones. Guitar part consists mostly of single-note phrases.

187 Frandsen, John. *Seven Silly Songs* (English). 1987/c1988 Reimers ER 101145. Mezzo F#3-F5/B3-E5. *D.* Group of seven songs (12'). Tonal with much chromaticism, featuring largely disjunct melodic motion and frequent meter changes. The text's humor is reinforced through such effects as senza vibrato, glissandi and whispering. Guitar part is varied and challenging.

188 Frandsen, John. *Songs of Experience* (English). 1991 composer. Text by William Blake. High B3-B5/D4-G5. *VD*. Group of five songs (12'). Atonal, with long, expressive phrases of varied motion; m7-M9 intervals common. Rhythms can be difficult due to frequent changes of often unusual meters (esp. song #5). Requires wide dynamic range and soft A5-B5. Quite varied in tempo and mood. Substantial guitar.

189 Frandsen, John. *Songs of Innocence* (English). 1984 Samfundet. Text by William Blake. High A3-B5/C#4-F#5. *VD*. Cycle of nine songs (18'). Atonal and often dissonant. Disjunct melodic motion with many large intervals (especially M7), yet often set in long, legato phrases. Numerous meter changes yielding difficult rhythm patterns. Widely varied moods. Difficult guitar part.

190 Fredriksson, Lennart. *Tre Sånger till Gitarr* (Swedish). 1979 Sweden T-2853. Text by various authors. High D4-G#5/E4-E5. *D*. Collection of three songs written over a period of 10 years. Tonal with chromaticism, featuring mostly stepwise melodic motion and uncomplicated rhythms. Varied in mood and tempo. Active, challenging guitar part.

191 Freedman, Harry. *Bright Angels*. 1995/c1995 Canada MV 1102 F853Br. Soprano B3-B5/Eb4-F#5. *VD*. Atonal vocalise features legato, disjunct, chromatic vocal lines; M7 leaps common. Ametrical yet rhythmically precise. Middle part is more animated and requires fortissimo sustained notes from G5 to B5. Austere guitar part is written on two staves, and was primarily designed to be played on lute.

192 Freedman, Harry. *Impromptus*. 1981/c1981 Canada MV 1102 F853im. Mezzo Ab3-G5/D4-E5. *VD*. Cycle of three songs (10'). Text consists solely of phonetic sounds. Atonal, frequently dissonant, with generally disjunct melodic motion. First song has frequent meter changes, but none of the songs has difficult rhythms. Active, varied guitar accompaniment.

193 Friberg, Tomas. *Ett Gult Rum* (Swedish). 1991 Sweden A-307. Text by Eva Runefelt. Soprano B3-B5/E4-F#5. *VD*. A "monologue for soprano and guitar" (7'30"). Atonal and dissonant, with much disjunct melodic motion featuring wide, chromatic intervals. Many complex rhythms and changing meters. Requires glissandi and sprechstimme. Guitar part is frequently difficult.

194 Fricker, Peter Racine. *O Mistress Mine* (English). 1961/c1963 Schott GA 210. Text by William Shakespeare. Tenor C3-G4/G3-G4. *M*. Diatonic with disjunct melodic motion containing numerous leaps of P4 and P5. Rhythms consist solely of eighth notes and quarter notes. Guitar part is lutelike, playing mostly lightly textured chords.

195 Fuchs, Stefan. *Malaisches Liebeslied* (German). 1978 composer. Text by Yvan Goll. Alto E3-D5/G3-A4. *D.* Atonal, with short, somewhat fragmented vocal lines that are often speech-like. Accessible chromatic melodic motion and rhythm in a *tranquillo* setting. Meters change frequently, especially in the beginning. Substantial, very active guitar is generally more prominent than the voice.

196 Fuchs, Stefan. *Sie Liebten Sich Beide* (German). 1979 composer. Text by Heinrich Heine. Alto A#3-G#5/B3-E4. *D.* Tonally elusive, with two brief, contrasting vocal phrases serving as recurring motives within the work, alternated with solo guitar passages in a largo tempo. Frequent meter changes, yet rhythms are generally accessible. Varied guitar part is often more prominent than the voice.

197 Gamberini, Leopoldo. *La Canzone del Galug* (Italian). c1995 Berben E. 3811 B. Text by Carlo Cormagi. Medium C4-G#5/E4-E5. *M.* Tonal, yet utilizes nontraditional harmonic sequences. Melodic motion is largely diatonic and stepwise, written in mostly long, legato phrases at an initial moderato tempo that gets progressively slower. Requires sustained fortissimo F5 and G#5. Accessible guitar often features parallel chords.

198 Garcia Morante, Manuel. *Siete Canciones* (Spanish). c1988 Catalana. Text by Juan Ramón Jiménez. Medium B3-E5/D4-D5. *D.* Group of seven songs (12') with clear Spanish folk characteristics in terms of melodic and rhythmic configurations. Varied musical moods demand a wide range of expressions from the singer. Active and challenging guitar part.

199 Gardner, Kay. *The Mother Songs* (English). c1976 composer. Text by composer. Low G3-D5/A3-A4. *E.* Group of two songs (5'). Diatonic with simple rhythms and melodies in strophic form. Texts are somewhat pastoral with a contemporary feminist perspective. Guitar part consists of simple accompanimental patterns which are repeated.

200 Gardner, Kay. *Two Sapphic Songs* (English). c1982 composer. Text by Elsa Gidlow. Mezzo E3-F5/A3-B4. *E.* Group of two songs (7'). Primarily diatonic with stepwise melodic motion. Contrasting moods; the first song is very lyrical and somewhat high, while the second is more fragmented and much lower in pitch. Simple, repetitive guitar accompaniment.

201 Gassul i Altisent, Feliu. *Sis Cançons* (Catalonian). 1987/c1989 Berben E. 3033 B. Text by Gabriel Ferrater from *Les Dones i els Dies*. Baritone G2-F#4/D3-E4. *VD.* Group of six songs (22'). Differing degrees of tonality in each piece, with colorful, often dissonant harmonies. Vocal phrases are moderately chromatic and generally long, with smooth melodic motion. Numerous uncommon meters. Expressive and emotionally varied. Challenging, substantial guitar.

202 Gefors, Hans. *Sånger om Förtröstan* (Swedish). 1972/c1992 Sweden Suecia 390. Text by Göran Tunström. Bass E2-G4/A2-E4. *M*. Group of four songs. Suggested time of 5' by composer seems short; more likely around 8'. Diatonic with stepwise motion and simple rhythms, often in contemporary folk style; the second piece is to be sung in the style of Bob Dylan. Written in tenor clef, but range implies a lower voice.

203 Gefors, Hans. *Sjöberg-Sånger* (Swedish). 1978 Sweden A-262. Text by Birger Sjöberg. Medium G3-G♭5/C4-D5. *D*. Cycle of three songs (12'). Tonal with some chromaticism. Mostly stepwise melodic motion. Rhythmically uncomplicated despite numerous meter changes. Frequent mood shifts, due largely to many changes in tempo. Active guitar part is varied and challenging.

204 Gentilucci, Armando. *Sparì la Luna* (Italian). 1985/c1985 Ricordi 133890. Text by Ugo Foscolo from *Frammento di Saffo*. Soprano C4-B5/E♭4-F5. *VD*. Atonal, featuring long, sometimes fragmented melismas of extremely disjunct melodic motion. Rhythmically complex and varied, ranging from long, sustained pitches to very rapid passages. Challenging guitar part is more linear than chordal.

205 Gerhard, Roberto. *Cantares* (Spanish). 1956/c1962 Mills MM 866. Text by various authors. High D4-G5/E4-E5. *D*. Group of seven Spanish folk songs (18') arranged in a more contemporary style, while preserving its traditional spirit. Features florid vocal ornaments and meter changes. Covers a wide spectrum of moods and tempi. Active, challenging, varied guitar part.

206 Gideon, Miriam. *Little Ivory Figures Pulled with a String* (English). 1959/c1959 ACA 6560. Text by Amy Lowell. Medium B♭3-A5/D4-F5. *D*. Vocal pitches and rhythms are frequently unspecified; only approximate pitches are given, indicated by solid horizontal lines on staff. Specific meter and tempi are likewise unspecified. Brief narrative section. Active guitar part.

207 Glanert, Detlev. *Drei Sonette* (German). c1993 Bote bb 1673. Text by Wolf Wondratschek. Baritone F♯2-F♯4/D3-E♭5. *VD*. Group of three songs (13'). Atonal and dissonant, with much disjunct melodic motion. Frequently changing meters and difficult rhythms. Dynamic levels are extreme and can alter abruptly. Falsetto, sprechstimme and glissandi are required. Difficult guitar part.

208 Glaser, Werner Wolf. *Ricordo*. 1972 Sweden T-2362. Medium A♭3-E5/D4-D5. *D*. Cycle of three songs (5'). No text given; the singer is free to sing any sound(s) desired. Tonal with chromaticism. Besides many stepwise melodic passages, there are sections of disjunct motion with very wide intervals. Meters change often, yet are rarely indicated.

209 Glasser, Stanley. *The Navigators* (English). c1981 Woza. Text by Adolph Wood. Baritone A♭2-F4/A2-E4. *VD.* Cycle of six songs with solo guitar interludes (20'). Atonal with unusual chromatic intervals and complex rhythms. Extended techniques include glissandi, shrieks, falsetto, sprechstimme and uncommon vowel sounds. The guitarist is also required to sing.

210 Gow, David. *Cantos Agridulces* (Spanish). Scotland. Text by Federico García Lorca. Mezzo A♭3-G#5/B3-E5. *D.* Group of five songs (12'30"). Chromatic, disjunct passages that are atonal in nature, yet repetitive and rhythmically uncomplicated, despite changing meters. Second song is a recitative, and the fourth is a cappella. Guitar part, mostly chordal, is not difficult.

211 Gow, David. *A Distant Room* (English). 1987 Scotland. Text by Thomas Hardy. Mezzo G#3-F#5/A3-E5. *D.* Cycle of five songs (14'). Atonal with much dissonance. Melodic motion is evenly balanced between stepwise and disjunct. Some meter changes, but rhythm is not complicated. Varied in tempo and mood. Guitar part has an optional cadenza-like ending in third song.

212 Grahn, Ulf. *2 Dagsedlar* (Swedish). 1971 Sweden T-0974. Text by Stig Dagerman. Medium A3-E5/A3-C5. *E.* Group of two strophic songs (2'30"). Diatonic with easy rhythms. Each song has its own distinctly different pitch range; the first is low (A3-F4), while the second is much higher (E4-E5). Simple, repetitive guitar accompaniment.

213 Greeson, James. *Three Poems by Stephen Crane* (English). c1983 Willis WMCo. 10824. Text by Stephen Crane. High D4-A5/E4-E5. *M.* Group of three songs (7'). The first and third songs are repetitive, diatonic, and rhythmically uncomplicated. The second piece is much faster (especially for guitar) and fragmented, with disjunct, chromatic melodic motion.

214 Gross, Eric. *Hark! Hark! The Lark!* (English). 1975/c1975 composer, also Australia Q783.66542/GRO7. Text by William Shakespeare from *Cymbeline.* Soprano E4-G5/E4-E5. *M.* Mostly diatonic with disjunct melodic motion, but intervals rarely exceed P4. Uncomplicated rhythms despite meter changes. Slow tempo and arpeggios in guitar accompaniment lend it a lute-like quality, befitting the historical ambience of the text.

215 Gross, Eric. *Lullaby* (English). 1965/c1965 composer, also Australia. Text by Alex Kitson. Soprano G#4-F#5/A4-E5. *E.* Simple, diatonic, legato melody and accompaniment which reinforce the serene nature of the text.

216 Guastavino, Carlos. *Pueblito, Mi Pueblo...* (Spanish). c1965 Ricordi S.A. BA12443. Text by Francisco Silva. Medium D4-C#5/D4-A4. *E.* Short, diatonic Spanish folk-style song in an *andante nostálgico* setting. Both rhythmic and melodic motives in both voice and guitar are quite repetitive and accessible. Active guitar acccompaniment.

217 Guastavino, Carlos. *Severa Villafañe* (Spanish). c1965 Ricordi S.A. BA12444. Text by Leon Benaros. Medium C4-E5/D4-D5. *M.* Diatonic strophic song in Spanish folk style. Features lively rhythms in 6/8 time, with numerous syncopations in both voice and guitar that are not difficult. Long vocal phrases of varied yet accessible melodic motion which are occasionally doubled by the guitar.

218 Guerrero, Francisco. *Erotica* (Arabic). 1978/c1984 Zerboni S. 8974 Z. Text by Benammed Abd Quzman. Medium G3-G#5/C4-E5. *VD.* Features extensive vocal ornamentation, thus giving a strong Eastern flavor. Highly detailed, complex rhythms for both voice and guitar, and likewise with the voice concerning dynamics.

219 Hallnäs, Hilding. *Maskinvisa* (Swedish). 1970 Sweden T-0150. Text by Nils Ferlin. High A3-G5/F#4-E5. *D.* Tonal with chromatic, disjunct melodic motion. Frequent meter changes, yet rhythmically uncomplicated. Ternary form. Guitar part consists mostly of rapid sixteenth-note passages.

220 Hallnäs, Hilding. *Molnet* (Swedish). 1978 Sweden T-2917. Text by Erik Johan Stagnelius. Medium B3-F#5/E4-D5. *M.* Primarily diatonic, with simple rhythms. Melodic leaps rarely exceed M3. Guitar part active and varied, yet not difficult.

221 Hallnäs, Hilding. *När Lyckan Mötte Kärleken* (Swedish). 1978 Sweden T-2291. Text by Nils Ferlin. High C4-F5/G4-E5. *M.* Mostly diatonic. Melodic line is well-balanced between stepwise and disjunct motion, with leaps no greater than M6. Uncomplicated rhythms with some meter changes. Guitar part is somewhat sparse and not difficult.

222 Hallnäs, Hilding. *När Skogens Källor Tystnat* (Swedish). 1968/c1968 Sweden T-2089. High C#4-F5/E4-E5. *M.* Tonal with chromaticism. Melody consists of a mixture of stepwise and disjunct motion, with several wide intervals. Uncomplicated rhythms despite meter changes. Long, continuous vocal lines at andantino tempo. Independent guitar part is not difficult.

223 Hallnäs, Hilding. *O Finns en Dag* (Swedish). 1974 Sweden T-2595. Text by Gunnar Björling. High C4-F#5/E4-E5. *M.* Little chromaticism or dissonance, yet tonality is elusive due to contemporary nature of the guitar harmonies (e.g., quartal chords). Long, sustained vocal lines with some disjunct motion. Guitar part is mostly chordal, readily supporting the vocal line.

224 Hallnäs, Hilding. *Visa* (Swedish). 1974 Sweden T-2596. Text by Reidar Ekner. Medium C#4-E5/E4-D5. *M.* Tonal with some chromaticism.

Animated vocal line with accessible rhythms and disjunct motion. Simple song structure. Active, varied guitar part is accessible to most players.

225 Hartikainen, Esko. *Kesällä Kerran* (Finnish). 1986/c1986 Finland 11452. Text by Veikko Ollikainen. Low G3-Aᵇ4/C4-G4. *E.* Simple, essentially strophic song in a slow tempo based on chord progressions found in popular music. Stepwise melodic motion and rhythm patterns consisting solely of either two eighth notes, or an eighth with two sixteenths. Folk-style guitar features arpeggiated chords in sixteenth notes.

226 Hartikainen, Esko. *Neljä Laulua Runebergin Runoihin* (Finnish). 1986/c1986 Finland 11461. Text by Johan Ludvig Runeberg. Medium A3-F5/B3-C#5. *E.* Group of four strophic songs. Tonal with traditional harmonies. Simple, straightforward melodies based on stepwise motion and basic rhythms. Consistent range of tempi throughout group (M.M. 66-76). Guitar part is comprised mostly of broken or block chords.

227 Hartikainen, Esko. *Nuku, Nuku Lapsi Pienoinen* (Finnish). 1988/c1988 Finland 12943. Text by Eirz Hartikainen. Low G3-A4/A3-E5. *E.* Simple, essentially strophic song in a moderate tempo based on chord progressions most readily found in popular music, with stepwise melodic motion and basic rhythm patterns. Guitar accompaniment consists almost exclusively of folk-style arpeggiated chords in eighth notes.

228 Hartzell, Eugene. *A Keats Songbook* (English). 1978/c1978 AMC M1624 H338 K5. Text by John Keats. Tenor D3-A4/F3-F4. *D.* Group of nine songs (27'). Tonal with much chromaticism, containing frequent melodic leaps and rapid melismas. Rhythms at times are demanding, due in part to numerous meter changes in several of the songs. Varied and challenging guitar part.

229 Haubenstock-Ramati, Roman. *Discours.* 1972/c1980 Ariadne 80034. Any voice range. *D.* (10-15'). Pictorial one-page music score, with no traditional notation used. No interpretive instructions or symbol definitions are provided.

230 Haubenstock-Ramati, Roman. *La Sonnambula.* 1972 Ariadne 80036. Any voice range. *D.* (10-15'). Pictorial one-page music score, with no traditional notation used. No interpretive instructions or symbol definitions are provided.

231 Heilner, Irwin. *Could Man Be Drunk Forever* (English). 1964/c1983 ACA E9307. Text by Alfred Edward Housman. Medium C4-D5/D4-D5. *M.* Diatonic with uncomplicated rhythms at a moderato tempo. Wide intervals such as P4, P5, and octaves are common, yet overall melodic motion is accessible. Guitar part often written on two treble clef staves. Originally written for voice and piano by composer.

232 Heilner, Irwin. *I Shall Not Care* (English). 1963/c1979 ACA 14664. Text by Sara Teasdale. Low G3-A4/G3-G4. *M.* Tonal with some chromaticism. Uncomplicated mixed melodic motion and rhythms, despite occasional changes into odd meters. Guitar part is often repetitive, containing accompanimental patterns of a contemporary folk nature.

233 Heilner, Irwin. *In Yalta* (English). 1983/c1983 ACA 10920. Text by I.E. Ranch. Tenor D3-G4/E3-E4. *D.* Tonal with chromaticism. Challenging rhythms due to frequent meter and tempo changes. Mostly disjunct melodic motion. Guitar part consists of primarily single-note passages, yet can be challenging, as in its brief cadenza.

234 Heilner, Irwin. *My Poems Are Full of Poison* (English). 1963/c1963 *Chelys* v.2 #4, also AMC 14676. Text by Heinrich Heine. Low A3-G4/A3-G4. *E.* Simple melody in strophic form. The guitar part is strictly accompanimental, consisting solely of Alberti bass-like patterns.

235 Heilner, Irwin. *Rock-'n'-Roll Session* (English). 1963/c1979 ACA 10655. Text by Phyllis McGinley from *Times Three.* Low G3-C5/A3-A4. *D.* Essentially diatonic with much disjunct melodic motion in a fast setting. Incorporates several meter changes which do not pose additional rhythm challenges. Humorous text. Active guitar part can be demanding at times.

236 Heilner, Irwin. *The Stars Have Not Dealt Me the Worst They Could Do* (English). 1964/c1983 ACA E9309. Text by Alfred Edward Housman. Medium C4-F5/F4-D4. *E.* Mostly diatonic melody with a folk-like unpretentious simplicity. Subtly humorous text. Accessible guitar part contains alternating sections; one consists primarily of single notes, while the other features chords.

237 Heilner, Irwin. *To the Guitarists* (English). 1978/c1978 ACA 14665. Text by Dober Spalding. High D4-A5/E4-E5. *D.* Tonal with chromaticism. Features changing meters and challenging rhythms. Some difficult vocal passages, most notably the rapid, high vocal melisma at the conclusion of the piece. Light-hearted text. Many fast guitar passages and frequent use of golpe.

238 Heilner, Irwin. *What Were They Like?* (English). 1968/c1968 ACA. Text by Denise Levertov. Medium B3-F#5/C4-D5. *M.* Primarily diatonic. Melody consists of an even balance between stepwise and disjunct motion, with intervals rarely exceeding P4. Somber text about Vietnamese peasants during the Vietnam conflict of the 1960s. Repetitive single-note guitar accompaniment uses harmonics often.

239 Heilner, Irwin. *Why the Soup Tastes Like the Daily News* (English). 1970/c1978 ACA 1496. Text by Marge Piercy from *Hard Loving.* Medium C4-D5/D5-A5. *M.* Topical, sarcastically humorous text. Tonal with uncomplicated rhythms. Melodic motion is largely accessible, yet there are several octave leaps featured. Guitar part is repetitive and accompanimental, consisting mostly of arpeggio configurations.

240 Heilner, Irwin. *The Wild Anemone* (English). 1968/c1968 *Chelys* v.2 #3, also ACA 10016. Text by James Laughlin. Medium B3-F5/B3-C5. *M.* Diatonic, with lyric, smooth vocal lines and uncomplicated rhythms in an adagio tempo. Accompanimental guitar part consists of repetitious sixteenth-note patterns which are of a contemporary folk nature in their structural simplicity.

241 Held, Wilbur. *A Mystic Song* (English). c1977 Beckenhorst. Medium E4-E5/E4-E5. *M.* Diatonic melody with both stepwise and disjunct motion that rarely exceeds P4. Melody consists of a six-measure motive which is repeated throughout with relatively uncomplicated variations in rhythm. Varied guitar part sometimes has contrasting rhythms.

242 Helmschrott, Robert M. *Atmosfera Ovattata III* (Italian). 1974/c198? Orlando. Soprano A3-C#6/B3-B♭5. *VD.* Atonal and unmetered, with rhythm notation given only to specify approximate durations. Improvisatory in nature. Contains extreme tessitura and dynamic levels. Wide vocal leaps and portamenti required. Complex, highly chromatic guitar part.

243 Henze, Hans Werner. *Drei Fragmente nach Hölderlin* (German). 1958/c1960 Schott ED 4886. Text by Friedrich Hölderlin from *In Lieblicher Bläue.* Tenor A#2-A4/E♭3-G4. *VD.* Cycle of three songs (12'), from Henze's *Kammermusik 1958.* Atonal with highly disjunct melodic motion. Many very long, legato vocal phrases with difficult and rapid rhythms. Dynamic levels of pianissimo and softer on high notes are common. Highly challenging guitar part.

244 Heyn, Thomas. *4 Aphorismen* (German). Neue NM 2015. Text by Achmatowa. High A3-B♭5/D4-G5. *VD.* Group of four songs (7'). Atonal, with disjunct and fragmented chromatic vocal phrases. Mostly uncomplicated rhythms in animated tempi. Song #1 is entirely spoken or whispered, and the guitar is solely percussive. Song #2 requires a sustained fortissimo B♭5. Song #4 features many soft descending phrases that begin on A♭5. Varied, often fragmented guitar part.

245 Heyn, Thomas. *Liebeslieder* (German). c1996 Margaux em 5103. Text by Andreas Reimann. Medium G3-A5/C4-E5. *VD.* Group of five songs (11'). Highly diverse degrees of tonality, chromaticism, melodic motion, and rhythms. Songs #2 & 4 solely contain spoken text over guitar music. Song #3 features very fast, tricky repetitive rhythms. Song #5 has wide leaps (up to P11) and several rapid chromatic melismas that span two octaves (A3-A5). Quite varied, often challenging guitar.

246 Hiatt, Kevin. *Four Songs from Chamber Music* (English). 1989/c1989 composer. Text by James Joyce from *Chamber Music*. Baritone A2-F#4/B2-D4. *D*. Group of four songs (12'). Songs vary greatly in their use of chromaticism, melodic motion, rhythm, tempo, dynamics. A wide range of moods, from gentle lyricism to powerful dramatics. Substantial guitar part can be quite challenging.

247 Hiatt, Kevin. *Holy Thursdays* (English). Composer. Text by William Blake. Tenor E3-B4/E3-G4. *VD*. Cycle of three songs (12'). Chromatic with much disjunct melodic motion. Long, connected vocal lines throughout. Frequent, sometimes complex meter changes. Requires sustained, powerful high notes. Varied in tempo and mood. Challenging guitar part.

248 Hildemann, Wolfgang. *Songs by Sir John* (English). 1993/c1994 Tonger 2633 P.J.T. Text by Sir John Suckling. Tenor Ab2-A4/D3-G4. *VD*. Group of three songs (10'). Atonal, with disjunct, fragmented melodic lines. Some difficult rhythms. Requires sprechstimme and breathy, murky low tones in first piece. Light-hearted text, yet tempi are generally slow. Fragmented guitar part can be challenging.

249 Hiller, Lejaren Arthur. *Five Appalachian Ballads* (English). 1958/c1978 Waterloo WCG-310. Medium Bb3-F5/D4-D5. *D*. Cycle of five songs (12'). Appalachian folk melodies coupled with an atonal, often dissonant guitar part that is rather elaborate and equally as important as the voice.

250 Hjelmborg, Bjørn. *Sprællemanden i Gadara* (Danish). 1976 composer. Text by Olov Hartmann. High or Medium D4-D5/E4-D5. *E*. Brief, lighthearted strophic song. Tonal with simple chromatic modulations that are strongly reinforced by the straightforward, consistent "oom-pah" guitar pattern. The accompaniment also alleviates the potential difficulties of several meter changes and unusual melodic intervals.

251 Hofmann-Engl, Ludger. *Am Eingang von Kotor* (German). 1988 composer. Text by Renate Fueß. Mezzo Ab3-A5/D4-E5. *D*. (10'). Sectionalized piece; among them there is one for guitar solo, and another for unaccompanied voice. Atonal, with several very wide vocal intervals. Utilizes sprechstimme and narration. Handwritten manuscript is often difficult to read.

252 Hol, Dirk. *Four Songs on Poems by Thomas Campion* (English). 1988/c1988 Donemus. Text by Thomas Campion. Medium C4-Gb5/E4-E5. *D*. Group of four songs (16'). Tonal with much chromaticism. Vocal lines often feature long, lyrical phrases with many unusual chromatic intervals. Varied in mood and tempo. Active and challenging guitar part.

253 Hold, Trevor. *Early One Morning* (English). 1966/c1975 Anglian ANMS 30. Text by Edward Thomas. Tenor Bb2-A4/D3-E4. *D*. Cycle of five songs (15'). Chromatic, with frequent wide melodic leaps. Intricate, often difficult rhythms and numerous unusual meter changes. Varied in tempo and mood. Text is often pastoral in nature. Some recitative sections. Active, varied guitar part.

254 Holmquist, Kay. *Lyrisk Cykel* (Swedish). 1987 composer. Text by Ingrid vom Trofimowitz. Soprano D4-B♭5/F4-E5. *D.* Cycle of five songs (13'). Mostly stepwise melodic motion. Not excessively chromatic, yet tonally ambiguous with frequent dissonances. Uncomplicated rhythms. Requires sustained, forte B♭5. Fourth song is notably faster than the others. Employs some unorthodox guitar sounds.

255 Hosokawa, Toshio. *Renka I* (Japanese). 1986/c1992 Schott Japan SJ 1066. Text by composer. Soprano G3-G♭5/B♭3-E♭5. *VD.* Cycle of three songs (13'). Text is presented via romanized Japanese with English translations. Avoidance of traditional Western tonality, along with frequent meter changes and complex rhythms in both parts is designed to help effect an Oriental chant.

256 Hübschmann, Werner. *Alte Deutsche Spruchweisheit* (German). 1963/c1973 DVfM 9044. Tenor C♯3-A4/E3-A4. *D.* Group of eight songs (12'), based on old German witticisms. Tonal with some chromaticism. Melodic motion is largely stepwise, yet wide leaps are not uncommon. Mostly consonant, although some melodies clash with the accompaniment. Accessible guitar part.

257 Hughes, Jerome. *David's Lament for Jonathan* (English). 1993/c1993 composer. Text by Peter Abelard. Tenor E3-G♭4/F♯3-E4. *M.* Tonal, beginning with mostly diatonic, smooth vocal phrases that become somewhat more chromatic and disjunct as the piece progresses, befitting the text's increasing anguish. Long, lyric melodies throughout with accessible rhythms set to a slow tempo. Subdued yet significant guitar part.

258 Hummel, Bertold. *Phantasus* (German). 1990/c1994 Vogt VF 1095. Text by Arno Holz. Medium A3-F5/D4-E5. *VD.* Cycle of six songs (20'). Atonal, with extensive chromaticism and disjunct melodic motion. Frequent meter changes, yet vocal rhythms are not excessively difficult. Nontraditional techniques include sprechstimme and guitar glissandi. Formidable, intricate guitar part.

259 Huyssen, Hans. *Die Stimmen* (German). 1992 composer. Text by Rainer Maria Rilke. Baritone F♯2-G4/A2-E4. *VD.* Cycle of seven songs (20'). First song is for guitar solo. The text of each song is about different social outcasts such as beggars, drunks, and idiots. Often dissonant and highly chromatic. Secure G4 required. Guitar part often written on multiple staves.

260 Huzella, Elek. *Four Love Songs* (Hungarian). c1975 Budapest 7405. Medium C4-E5/E4-D5. *E.* Group of four short strophic songs (5') with a distinctive Hungarian folk flavor due to the use of harmonic minor scales and half cadences. Interesting, accessible guitar part occasionally extends beyond straightforward chordal accompaniment.

261 Iglesia, Gérard. *D—Rives...* (French). 1991 composer. Text by composer. Baritone G2-F4/B2-C4. *VD.* Cycle of four songs (10'). Atonal and dissonant, with often fragmented vocal phrases of disjunct chromatic motion. Many intricate rhythms in changing, unspecified meters set to moderate to very slow tempi. Dynamics rarely louder than mezzo piano. Varied guitar part calls for many diverse timbres.

262 Jacobsen, Odd-Arne. *Vocalise.* 1983 Norway S 400 JAC. Mezzo A3-G♯5/F♯4-E5. *D.* A vocalise that is tonally elusive, yet contains many chords associated with popular music and jazz. Vocal line is often chromatic and varied in melodic motion, with long, legato phrases. Meter changes and challenging rhythms in a relaxed adagio. Accessible guitar is largely chordal in design.

263 Jalkanen, Pekka. *Kreikkalaisia Lauluja I-III* (Finnish). 1980/c1980 Finland 6600. Text by Pentti Saarikoski. Medium or Low A3-D5/C4-D♭5. *VD.* Group of three songs (10'). Atonal and ametrical, with mixed chromatic melodic motion that rarely features intervals wider than P5. Generally long vocal phrases of varied, short rhythm divisions. No tempi given. Handwritten notation is often difficult to read. Difficult guitar.

264 Johanson, Björn. *Det Glädjerika Regnets Lövsal* (Swedish). 1975 Sweden A-47. Text by various authors. High or Medium B3-F♯5/D4-E5. *D.* (18'). Elusive tonality, with many different sections varying in tempo, meter, key, and melodic and harmonic structure. Generally long, relatively smooth chromatic melodic motion with uncomplicated rhythms. Several accompanied and unaccompanied recitative sections. Guitar part is written mostly for the lute, and often has a sparse, transparent texture.

265 Johanson, Bryan. *Four American Songs* (English). 1984/c1984 *Soundboard* #20 v.4 and #21 v.1. Medium C4-E5/D4-D5. *M.* Group of four traditional American folk songs (10'), newly arranged. Varied in mood and tempo. The accessible guitar part is based on conventional harmonies, yet uses "color" tones (i.e., M6 and M7), harmonics and different accompaniment patterns to create variety.

266 Johansson, Gunde. *Omkring Tiggarn Från Luossa* (Swedish). c1971 Zindermans. Text by Dan Andersson. Medium G3-D5/A3-B4. *E.* Collection of 15 songs. Diatonic songs of a contemporary folk nature in their melodic simplicity. Guitar parts are texturally sparse and easily playable.

267 Jong, Marinus de. *Bruegel-liederen* (Dutch). c1969 Belgium. Text by Bert Peleman. Baritone G2-G4/D3-D4. *D*. Cycle of seven songs (20'). Tonal with much chromaticism. Rhythms not difficult despite meter changes. Wide array of tempi and moods. Guitar part is quite varied, ranging from simple, slow chords to fast, highly challenging sections.

268 Jung, Helge. *Das Holzhaus* (German). c1980 Neue NM 430. Text by Johannes Robert Becher. Low F3-A♭4/G3-E4. *D*. From the 11-song collection *Ich Liebe Dich*, compiled by Sonja Kehler. Somewhat chromatic; more so in guitar. Nontraditional harmonies make tonality elusive. Largely stepwise melodic motion set to varying, speech-like rhythms. Mostly chordal guitar part.

269 Jung, Helge. *Lied vom Anderssein* (German). c1971 Neue NM 430. Text by Johannes Robert Becher. Alto D3-D5/A3-C5. *D*. From the 11-song collection *Ich Liebe Dich*, compiled by Sonja Kehler. Also found in Neue NM 285 (see entry #346). Mostly diatonic with stepwise melodic motion and simple rhythms. Written in tenor clef, but the tessitura of the middle section is extremely high (A4-D5), implying alto voice.

270 Jung, Helge. *Das Schneegesicht* (German). c1980 Neue NM 430. Text by Johannes Robert Becher. Tenor G3-A♭4/B♭3-G4. *D*. From the 11-song collection *Ich Liebe Dich*, compiled by Sonja Kehler. Somewhat chromatic; the often nonfunctional guitar harmonies are frequently dissonant with the melody. Sustained legato lines around the passaggio. Varied, active guitar part.

271 Katzer, Georg. *Ach, Dummes Herz* (German). c1980 Neue NM 430. Text by Johannes Robert Becher. Tenor F3-A4/A3-F♯4. *M*. From the 11-song collection *Ich Liebe Dich*, compiled by Sonja Kehler. Tonal with some chromaticism, featuring much disjunct melodic motion. Frequent meter changes, yet accessible rhythms. Requires use of sprechstimme. Active guitar accompaniment.

272 Katzer, Georg. *Hoch Über der Stadt* (German). c1980 Neue NM 430. Text by Johannes Robert Becher. Medium A3-B4/B3-A4. *E*. From the 11-song collection *Ich Liebe Dich*, compiled by Sonja Kehler. Diatonic with simple rhythms and stepwise melodic motion. Guitar part is technically quite accessible and accompanimental in nature.

273 Keam, Glenda. *Two Spanish Songs* (Spanish). Composer. Text by various authors. Soprano C4-A♭5/E4-F♯5. *D*. Group of two songs (5'). Atonal with chromatic, frequently disjunct melodic motion that is often dissonant to the guitar. Vocal rhythms are challenging due to numerous syncopations, unusual time signatures (song #2 is in 7/8), and the independent, varied, and demanding guitar part.

274 Kingman, Daniel C. *Songs of Solitude and Exultation* (English). c1987 composer. Text by Robert Bly. Soprano B♭3-B♭5/D4-F♯5. *VD.* Cycle of 17 songs (25'), which include within *Five Meditations for Solo Guitar.* Widely varied in the use of chromaticism, melodic motion, rhythm and mood throughout the entire cycle, as implied by the work's title. Challenging, substantial guitar part.

275 Klein, Richard Rudolf. *Das Männlein in der Gans* (German). c1988 Vogt V&F 409. Text by Friedrich Ruckert. Medium D4-G5/E4-E5. *M.* Group of two songs (7'). Uncomplicated rhythms and largely stepwise diatonic melodies. Both songs are fairly fast and feature mostly eighth notes and quarter notes, with few sustained pitches. Very accessible, straightforward guitar accompaniment.

276 Knopf, Michael. *The Fleeting Hours of Man's Life* (English). Composer, also Australia. Text by Abdul-Baha. Medium C4-E5/F4-E♭5. *D.* Little traditional harmony is used, but continuous pitch references imply a tonal center. Chromatic vocal line is often dissonant to guitar, yet has uncomplicated melodic motion and rhythms. Contemplative, religious text builds to powerful climax. Accessible, often repetitive guitar part.

277 Knopf, Michael. *Three Songs from the Hidden Words* (English). 1993/c1993 composer, also Australia 783.2525/KNO2-4. Text by Bahá ú lláh from *Hidden Words.* Medium B♭3-F5/E4-E5. *D.* Group of three songs (10'). Essentially tonal with chromaticism. Much stepwise melodic motion interspersed with disjunct sections. Some passages of long, sustained notes require good breath control. Rhythmically uncomplicated. Active, often repetitive guitar part.

278 Koepf, Siegfried. *Module.* 1992/c1992 Feedback FB 9023. Any voice range. *D.* Chance composition for any two players. Involves performing intervallic "modules." Directions give little emphasis to timbre, dynamics, or rhythm. Score consists of 25 blocks—every other one notes a module to be performed. The others are blank, allowing performers to freely choose a module.

279 Kölz, Ernst. *Donauballade* (German). 1960 composer. Text by Else Kölz from *War es Mord?.* Medium or Low B3-B4/E4-A4. *E.* Short, strophic song of five verses in E minor. Diatonic with simple, repetitive melody and rhythms. Guitar accompaniment consists solely of eighth-note "oom-pah" chordal configurations.

280 Kölz, Ernst. *Pseudochinesische Lieder* (German). 1988 composer, also Robitschek. Text by Klabund. High or Medium C4-G5/E4-D5. *D.* Cycle of five short songs (5'), of which the first and last are virtually identical. Each song is based either on pentatonic or whole tone scales, with resulting harmonies. Uncomplicated melodies and accompaniments that are often highly repetitious. Generally slow tempi throughout.

281 Kölz, Ernst. *Sonett* (German). 1979 composer. Text by William Shakespeare. Any voice range C#4-B4/E4-A4. *E.* Tonal, with chromaticism common in minor keys. Vocal line, often consisting of repeated pitches or stepwise chromatic motion, is strongly supported by the exclusively chordal guitar accompaniment. Simple yet varied rhythms and meter within the piece.

282 Komter, Jan Maarten. *In a Gondola* (English). 1946/c1963 Donemus. Text by Robert Browning. Soprano E4-E5/F#4-E5. *E.* Diatonic, strophic song with simple melodic motion and rhythms. Long, connected vocal phrases and simple, largely chordal guitar accompaniment yields a tranquil and unpretentious effect.

283 Konietzny, Heinrich. *Kalypso* (German). 1973/c1976 Trekel T 649. Medium B3-G♭5/C4-D5. *VD.* (7'). Atonal with detached, highly disjunct melodic motion featuring many unusual chromatic intervals. Intricate and varied rhythms. Described as a "scene," the work features several sections largely denoted by changes in tempo. Demanding and very active guitar part.

284 Kruisbrink, Annette. *Harmony* (English). 1990 composer. Text by composer. High B3-A♭5/E4-E5. *D.* Tonal with chromaticism. Mostly disjunct melodic motion with a few unusual chromatic intervals. Intimate, romantic text set to speech-like rhythms at a moderate tempo. Requires soft, legato A5 and A♭5. Active, varied guitar part is frequently most prominent.

285 Kruisbrink, Annette. *Hij of Zij* (Dutch). 1996/c1996 composer. Text by Hans Lodeizen. High C#4-A5/D4-E5. *D.* Cycle of six songs (12'). Tonally ambiguous, yet does not use extensive chromaticism. Accessible melodic motion and rhythms, in tempi ranging from slow to moderate. Songs #1-3 are ametrical, and #4 & 5 feature simple meter changes. Frequently repetitive guitar motives are often not difficult, and help to set the mood of each song.

286 Kruse, Bjørn. *Islys* (Norwegian). 1990 Norway. Text by Stein Mehren. Soprano C4-A♭5/D4-F5. *D.* (9'). Tonal, but often elusive due to much dissonance. Many long, legato phrases. Melodic motion ranges from smooth melismas to wide leaps exceeding an octave. Varied rhythms and dynamics are sometimes challenging. Middle section features ametrical, somewhat improvisatory passages.

287 Kubizek, Augustin. *Altdeutsche Weihnachtslieder* (German). 1986 composer. High D4-A5/E4-E5. *M.* Group of 12 old German Christmas songs (30') with revised accompaniments. With the exception of songs #6 & 7, which respectively feature high tessitura and long melismas, all are very easy to sing. Accessible guitar is traditional in structure, yet features some contemporary harmonies.

288 Kukuck, Felicitas. *Ich Hab die Nacht Geträumet* (German). c1968 Möseler M 59.307. Text from various 19th-century poems. High B3-G5/E4-E5. *E.* Group of seven songs (10'), of which the third is for solo guitar. Described as "mädchenlieder" (maiden songs), the set features diatonic, strophic pieces that are folk-like in their melodic, rhythmic, and accompanimental simplicity.

289 **Kukuck,** Felicitas. *Ten Liebeslieder* (German). c1985 Möseler M 24.851. Text by Margret Johannsen. Soprano B3-A5/D4-E5. *M.* Group of 10 songs (18'). Mostly strophic, diatonic songs with straightforward melodies and uncomplicated rhythms. Several songs call for dramatically sung high notes. Guitar part, while active, is primarily accompanimental in nature.

290 Kulp, Jonathan. *Alone* (English). 1994/c1994 composer. Text by James Joyce from *Pomes Penyeach.* High D4-A5/E4-F#5. *D.* Atonal, yet dissonances are not extensive. Much smooth, lyrical melodic motion. Uncomplicated rhythms in a serene *adagio solitario* setting. Varied guitar part features several brief melodies via harmonics, and is integral to the work, being equally significant as the voice part.

291 Kulp, Jonathan. *Penelope (or, "Molly's Reverie")* (English). 1994/c1994 composer. Text by James Joyce from *Ulysses.* Soprano E4-A5/G4-F5. *D.* (8'). Tonally elusive, with somewhat chromatic yet smooth melodic phrases. Text deals with a woman's erratic thoughts about her troubled marriage and consequent adultery. Varied speech-like vocal rhythms and tempi. Guitar part is largely accompanimental, using various patterns that are repeated

292 **Kulp,** Jonathan. *Remanso. Canción Final* (Spanish). 1995/c1995 composer. Text by Federico García Lorca from *Remansos.* High G4-G5/B4-G5. *M.* Guitar introduction is dissonant and tonally ambiguous. The music then becomes much more tonal in the four strophic verses and coda. Smooth, long vocal lines. Simple rhythms in both parts. Strong, dramatically sustained G5 near end. Accessible guitar is largely accompanimental in nature. May be added as a fourth song to composer's *Tres Canciones para Niños* (see entry #294).

293 Kulp, Jonathan. *Three Poems of James Joyce* (English). 1991/c1994 composer. Text by James Joyce from *Collected Poems.* Medium Bb3-F5/D4-D5. *D.* Group of three songs (8'). Chromatic tonality with recurrent dissonances. Melodic motion is frequently disjunct, yet its uncomplicated rhythms and accessible intervals yield a lyrical quality. Varied in tempo and mood. Active and challenging guitar part.

294 **Kulp,** Jonathan. *Tres Canciones para Niños* (Spanish). 1994/c1994 composer. Text by Federico García Lorca from *Canciones para Niños.* High E4-A5/B4-G#5. *D.* Group of three songs (8'). Mostly accessible melodic motion and rhythms, often reminiscent of Spanish folk song. Guitar largely consists of repeated accompanimental figures that are often tonally ambiguous. Varied in tempo and mood. Some consistently high passages, sometimes dramatically sung. Also see entry #292.

295 Kunad, Rainer. *Schattenland Ströme* (German). 1966/c1968 DVfM 9041. Text by Johannes Bobrowski. Tenor C3-B4/G3-G4. *VD.* Cycle of 10 songs (20'), 3 of which are for solo guitar. Atonal with much highly disjunct melodic motion. Fragmented voice and guitar lines. Frequent meter changes and extreme dynamic levels. Some glissando and sprechstimme required. Varied guitar part.

296 Kunad, Rainer. *Von der Kocherie* (German). 1970/c1973 DVfM 9046. High E4-B5/F4-F5. *VD.* Cycle of 14 songs (20'). Tonally elusive with some dissonance. Light-hearted text about food and old recipes. Rhythms are generally not difficult. Varied in mood and musical setting. Requires trills, coloratura, sprechstimme and glissandi. Many declamatory phrases.

297 Kupferman, Meyer. *The Red Sand Beneath Us* (English). 1990/c1990 Virtuoso 9012. Text by composer. Tenor C3-A4/D3-F4. *VD.* Frequent meter and tempo changes. Several nonmetered "free" sections. Highly chromatic and atonal with disjunct melodic passages for both voice and guitar. Wide array of moods (e.g., misterioso, agitato, tranquillo), often changing abruptly.

298 Kutzer, Ernst. *Drei Lieder* (German). c1985 Preissler JP 70210. Text by Otto Molz. Medium B3-E5/E4-D5. *M.* Group of three songs (7'). Diatonic, with mostly stepwise melodic motion and uncomplicated, repetitive rhythms. Varied in tempo. Accessible guitar part is essentially chordal in design and accompanimental in nature.

299 Kutzer, Ernst. *Düstere Fahrt* (German). c198? Preissler JP 70214. Text by Erich Ludwig Biberger. Low G3-E♭5/D4-D5. *M.* Group of five songs (10'). Mostly diatonic and well balanced between stepwise and simple disjunct melodic motion. Uncomplicated, often repetitive rhythms. Wide array of tempi and moods. Tessitura may be better suited to a medium voice. Active, substantial guitar part.

300 Kutzer, Ernst. *Fünf Lieder, Op. 73* (German). c1988 Preissler JP 70217. Text by Ernst R. Hauschka. Medium B3-F5/E4-E5. *M.* Group of five songs (8'). Diatonic with stepwise melodic motion and straightforward rhythms. Relatively little variation in mood or tempo. Guitar part largely consists of accompanimental patterns which are repeated through each song.

301 Kutzer, Ernst. *Fünf Lieder, Op. 93* (German). c1985 Preissler JP 70211. Text by Peter Coryllis. Medium G3-E5/C4-E5. *M.* Group of five songs (10'). Tonal with chromaticism. Somewhat disjunct yet accessible melodic motion with simple rhythms. Varied in mood and tempo. Active, substantial guitar part is prominently featured and of moderate difficulty.

302 Kutzer, Ernst. *Des Jahres Saitenspiel* (German). c1988 Preissler JP 70218. Text by Liesl Breitfelder. Medium D4-E5/E4-D5. *E.* Group of six songs (12'). Strophic songs of folk-like melodic simplicity. Guitar part features repetitious accompaniment patterns which vary from piece to piece.

303 Kutzer, Ernst. *Six Songs* (German). c1985 Preissler JP 70212. Text by various authors. Medium A3-E5/C4-D5. *M.* Group of six songs (12'). Mostly diatonic with mixed yet uncomplicated melodic motion and repetitive rhythm patterns. Somewhat varied in mood and tempi. Accessible, active guitar part is mostly chordal in design and accompanimental in nature.

304 Kutzer, Ernst. *Vier Lieder* (German). c198? Preissler JP 70215. Text by Ursula Student. Medium D4-G5/E4-E5. *M.* Group of four songs (10'). Tonal with accessible, lyric melodies that frequently require secure, strong pitches at the top of the staff. Varied guitar part interacts well with the voice.

305 Kverno, Trond. *En Bibelsk Visebok* (Norwegian). 1972/c1976 Norsk NMO 8941. Text by various authors. High or Medium B3-E5/D4-D5. *E.* Group of seven sacred strophic songs (10'). Simple, almost exclusively diatonic melodies and accompaniment. Very accessible rhythms except for song #6, which alternates between 7/4, 3/2, and 5/4. Guitar part is mostly chordal. Some songs allow for extra melodic instruments (optional).

306 Landeghem, Jan Van. *Drie Erotische Liedekens* (Dutch). 1995 Belgium 96.202. Text by Beatrijs van Craenenbroeck. Soprano D4-C#6/E4-E5. *VD.* Group of three songs (7'). Atonal with disjunct, chromatic melodies. Intricate, varied rhythms amidst changing meters and moods. Songs #2 and #3 feature melismas and fortissimo high notes (A♭5-C#6), often sustained. Sprechstimme, glissandi, clapping, and many percussive guitar effects are required.

307 Lauré, Orvar. *Sex Kärlekssånger* (Swedish). Sweden T-3355. Text by Ture Nerman. High or Medium G3-F#5/E4-D5. *M.* Group of six songs (12'). Mostly diatonic with varied, accessible melodic motion, rhythms, and tempi. Song #6 features 12/8 accompaniment while the voice is in 4/4. Both guitar and piano are included, but songs #4 & 6 do not provide a guitar part. Song #2 is notably lower (G3-G4 tessitura) than the others. Varied yet uncomplicated guitar.

308 Lauré, Orvar. *Sex Poeters Visor* (Swedish). Sweden A-319. Text by various authors. High or Medium D4-F5/D4-F5. *E.* Group of six songs (14'). Simple, repetitive melodies with straightforward guitar accompaniments (a piano version is also provided). Song #2, which is strophic, may be sung a cappella. Song #4 has a very brief spoken ending. Several songs feature tempo changes within.

309 Lauré, Orvar. *Det Var en Hjärtens Dag* (Swedish). Sweden A-318.
Text by various authors. High or Medium C4-F#5/D4-D5. *M*. Group of seven
songs (14'). Mostly diatonic with accessible and often repetitive melodies and
rhythms. Songs #1 & 7 are strophic. Both guitar and piano are included, but
songs #3 & 5 do not provide a guitar part. Varied yet straightforward, uncomplicated guitar accompaniments.

310 Lauridsen, Morten. *Dirait-on* (French). 1993/c1995 Peer. Text by
Rainer Maria Rilke from *Les Roses*. High C4-Bᵇ5/F4-F5. *M*. Diatonic, with
very accessible melodic motion and rhythms set to long, legato phrases in a
relaxed moderato tempo. Should be performed with much rubato. Arranged
from the original voice/piano score based on the composer's choral piece *Les
Chansons des Roses*. Accessible guitar part.

311 Lee, Noël. *Three Songs from Shakespeare* (English). c1992 composer.
Text by William Shakespeare. Medium B3-Aᵇ5/F#4-F#5. *D*. Group of three
songs (10'). Atonal with many dissonances. Melodic motion is generally disjunct, with some difficult intervals. Rhythmically uncomplicated and frequently lyric. Widely varied moods and tempi. Tessitura more suitable for a
high voice.

312 Lehrman, Leonard. *A March for Ben & Mary Beth* (English).
1983/c1983 composer. Text by Mary Beth Armes. High D4-Aᵇ5/D4-Aᵇ5. *D*.
Very short song (30") featuring mostly chromatic melodic motion in an atonal
setting. The piece alternates between rhythmic, march-like sections and sustained, legato phrases. Requires a crescendo from piano to forte on sustained
high notes.

313 Lehrman, Leonard. *Sonnetina #6* (English). 1982/c1982 composer.
Text by e.e. cummings. Baritone C2-Gᵇ4/G2-F4. *VD*. Atonal with highly disjunct melodic motion consisting of many wide intervals (M6 or larger). Many
meter changes, yet rhythms are not complicated. Numerous high pitches.
Extremely low tones may be sung octave higher. Guitar part consists mostly
of single notes.

314 Lehrman, Leonard. *Spiele* (German). 1980/c1980 composer. Text
by Peter Maiwald. Medium Bᵇ3-G5/D4-D5. *VD*. Extremely fast piece in
5/4 (M.M. 205). Atonal, with melodic motion well-balanced between stepwise and disjunct motion, the latter sometimes consisting of very wide intervals. Rhythms are mostly quarter notes and half notes. Difficult, rapid guitar
part.

315 Leisner, David. *Confiding* (English). 1985/c1985 composer. Text by
various women authors. High C4-A5/E4-G5. *D*. Cycle of 10 songs (25').
Tonal with some chromaticism. A balanced combination of stepwise and
accessibly disjunct melodic motion. Generally uncomplicated rhythms. Quite

varied in terms of mood; some sections are very dramatic. Substantial, active guitar part.

316 Leisner, David. *Five Songs of Devotion* (English). 1989/c1994 Columbia CO 338. Text by various authors. Medium C4-F5/C4-D5. *M.* Group of five songs (16') of diverse spiritual perspectives. Mostly diatonic with varied yet uncomplicated melodic motion. The third song briefly features unusual meter changes; otherwise, rhythm is quite accessible. Guitar part often accompanimental in nature.

317 Leisner, David. *Four Yiddish Songs* (Yiddish). 1983/c1983 composer. Text by various authors. Medium C4-F5/E4-E5. *M.* Group of four songs (12'). Traditional Yiddish melodies set to contemporary accompaniments. Diatonic, with simple rhythms and mostly stepwise melodic motion. Incorporates traditional idioms such as accelerandi and improvisation. Accessible guitar part.

318 Leisner, David. *Heaven's River* (English). 1991/c1991 composer. Text by Rabindranath Tagore from *Gitanjali*. Soprano E4-A5/E4-F#5. *D.* Cycle of three songs (12'). Tonal with some chromaticism. Varied yet mostly uncomplicated melodic motion. Some meter changes, notably in the second song where 4/4 and 6/8 frequently alternate. Varied in tempo and expression. Some very rapid sections in guitar.

319 Leisner, David. *O Love Is the Crooked Thing* (English). 1980/c1980 composer. Text by William Butler Yeats. Low F#3-E5/A3-D5. *D.* Cycle of five songs (15'). Tonal with primarily stepwise, sometimes chromatic melodic motion. Varied rhythmically, with some songs featuring intricate subdivisions. A wide array of dynamics, tempi and moods. Expressive, active guitar part can be challenging.

320 Leisner, David. *Outdoor Shadows* (English). 1985/c1986 Merion 141-40018. Text by Robert Francis from *Collected Poems, 1936-1976*. High D4-B5/E4-F5. *D.* Cycle of five songs (12'). Primarily diatonic. Vocal line is largely stepwise; leaps are rarely wider than P5. Long, continuous vocal passages are common, and strong, sustained A5 and B5 are present. Fourth song is somewhat ametrical, and fifth song is in 7/4.

321 Leisner, David. *Simple Songs* (English). 1982/c1984 AMP 79003. Text by Emily Dickinson. Medium B3-G♭5/E4-E5. *D.* Cycle of six short songs (10'). Widely varied in terms of technical demands and difficulty. Songs #1 and #2 would be accessible to most singers, song #3 features many wide leaps (M7 and M9), song #4 has intricate speech-like rhythms, and song #5 is virtually a cappella.

322 Lendle, Wolfgang. *Cinco Canciones Populares Ecuatoria* (Spanish). c1992 Margaux em 5102. Mezzo A3-G#5/D4-F5. *M.* Group of five songs

(12'). Melodies and text from traditional Spanish songs. Diatonic with varied, simple melodic motion. Some unusual features, such as the mostly 5/8 meter mixed with 3/4 and 6/8 in the third song. Straightforward guitar accompaniment.

323 Levin, Gregory. *Come Away, Death* (English). c1978 Canada MV 1102 L665co. Text by William Shakespeare from *Twelfth Night.* Medium D4-E5/E4-E5. *M.* Diatonic with mostly stepwise melodic motion. Numerous syncopated rhythms in voice part. Frequent, somewhat abrupt dynamic changes. Guitar part is texturally sparse, yielding a lute-like sound.

324 Levin, Gregory. *O Mistress Mine* (English). c1978 Canada MV 1102 L665om. Text by William Shakespeare from *Twelfth Night.* Tenor E3-G4/F#3-E4. *M.* Tonal with some chromaticism. Largely disjunct melodic motion; wider intervals such as m7 and M7 occur regularly. Rhythms consist solely of half notes and quarter notes. Frequent dynamic changes. Mostly chordal guitar accompaniment is very accessible.

325 Liani, Davide. *Cjantis* (Friulian). c1983 Zanibon G. 6043 Z. Text by various authors. High or Medium D4-F#5/F#4-D5. *M.* Group of three strophic songs (6'). Diatonic, with very simple, folk-like repetitive phrases. First two songs use changing meters; song #1 has sections of 7/8. Friulian is a dialect mixture of Northern Italian and Yugoslavian. Guitar part is quite accessible, consisting solely of chords.

326 Lilburn, Douglas. *Sings Harry* (English). 1954/c1991 Waiteata 1991 #44. Text by Dennis Glover. Tenor D3-A4/E3-E4. *M.* Cycle of six songs (11'10"). Primarily diatonic with varied yet accessible melodic motion. Rhythm patterns, while generally not difficult, frequently vary. Text is introspective and sometimes nostalgic, and each song ends with the words "Sings Harry."

327 Luff, Enid. *Spring Bereaved* (English). 1976/c1980 Primavera. Text by William Drummond. Baritone C3-F#4/E3-E4. *D.* Cycle of three songs (12'), each untitled. Atonal with frequent dissonances. Predominantly stepwise, chromatic motion with some wider yet accessible leaps. Many meter changes, yet not difficult rhythmically. All three songs maintain a moderato tempo and mood.

328 Lundén, Lennart. *Överdrivna Ord* (Swedish). 1964/c1964 Ehrling ES 3082. Text by Birger Sjöberg from *Fridas Tredje Bok.* Medium C4-E5/D4-D5. *M.* Group of seven strophic songs (20'). Mostly diatonic and folk-like in terms of its rhythmic, melodic, and formal simplicity. Last song is in 5/4. Notable contrast in tempo between each song. Varied guitar part is not difficult and often accompanimental in nature.

329 Lundén, Lennart. *Tio Visor* (Swedish). 1965/c1966 Ehrling TE 576. Text by Alf Henriksons from *Medan Göken Tiger.* Medium B3-D5/D4-D5.

M. Group of 10 short songs (15'). Mostly diatonic with much stepwise melodic motion and uncomplicated rhythms. Somewhat varied in mood and tempi. Guitar part is technically accessible and often accompanimental in nature.

330 Lunn, John. *Ethic of White* (English). 1982 Scotland. Text by composer. Tenor D3-B4/E3-G4. *VD*. Atonal in nature, yet not extensively chromatic. Vocal line often disjunct and fragmented, with intricate rhythms and frequent meter changes. Incorporates sprechstimme and laughing. Disjointed text of topical racial/social concerns. Active, difficult guitar.

331 Lutyens, Elizabeth. *By All These....* (English). 1977/c1988 Olivan. Text by Richard Jefferies. Soprano G#3-C6/E4-F5. *VD*. (7'). Atonal and unmeasured, with highly disjunct, chromatic melodic motion and often complex rhythm patterns. Frequent, extreme dynamic changes at all pitch levels. Both voice and guitar parts are quite fragmented. Sparse yet difficult guitar passages.

332 Lyne, Peter. *Two Love Poems* (English). 1976 Sweden T-2683. Text by Ena Hollis. High E4-A5/G4-G5. *D*. Group of two songs (5'). Chromatic and melodically disjunct. The slow first song is mostly arhythmic with only relative duration values (e.g., short, long) given, yielding an improvisatory mood. The second song is fast and rhythmic with unusual meter changes.

333 Macbride, David. *Wanderer* (English). 1980/c1980 ACA 14773. Text by Pai Ch'iu. Baritone G#2-F#4/D3-Eb4. *D*. From the composer's one-act opera *The Pond in a Bowl*, pp. 4-7. Frequent meter changes or no meter. One section requires singer to mouth words in silence, thinking of the given pitches. Guitar part contains abrupt dynamic changes in rapid passages.

334 McCombe, Christine. *Halcyon* (English). 1994/c1994 composer. Text by Christina Rossetti. Soprano A3-E5/E4-C#5. *D*. Cycle of three songs (8'). Song #1 is tonal, with repeated accessible patterns in both parts. Other songs are atonal; rhythmically complex, they consist of disjunct, fragmented chromatic vocal lines over dissonant, ever-varying guitar. Slow tempi throughout. Range perhaps best suited for mezzo.

335 MacDonald, Andrew Paul. *Songs of the Wind Among the Reeds* (English). 1983/c1984 New Art. Text by William Butler Yeats. Soprano A#3-A5/E4-F5. *VD*. Cycle of three songs (15'). Highly chromatic, atonal setting with many dissonances between voice and guitar. Frequently disjunct melodies, yet phrases often long and lyrical in design. Numerous changes in meter and rhythm configurations. Substantial, challenging guitar part.

336 Malipiero, Riccardo. *Due Ballate* (German). 1965/c1965 Zerboni S. 6480 Z. Text by various authors. Mezzo G3-A5/D4-F5. *D*. Cycle of two untitled songs (9'). Atonal with many uncommon and large melodic leaps.

Rhythmically challenging, due partly to frequent meter changes. Demanding, varied guitar part.

337 Marco, Tomás. *Luar* (Spanish). 1991/c1991 Santiago. Text by Rosalía de Castro from *En las Orillas* and *Cantares gallegos*. High E4-A5/E4-E5. *D.* (8'). From Volume 5 of *Cuadernos de "Música en Compostela."* Tonal with repetitive, legato melodies. Largely stepwise melodic motion, yet A3 and A4 intervals are common, as are rapid, grupetto-like passages and glissandi. Humming is predominant in sections. Active guitar yields varied moods.

338 Marina, Carmen. *Canción Incredula (Bolero)* (Spanish). 1974/c1978 *Chelys* v.2 #3. Text by R. de Montesinos. Mezzo A♭3-C♯5/A♭3-A4. *M.* Diatonic with accessible melodic motion through several key changes. Features many characteristics of Spanish music, most prominent of which are the bolero-like rhythm patterns. Active guitar part consists of accompanimental chords and arpeggios.

339 Marina, Carmen. *Lyric* (English). 1976/c1978 *Chelys* v.2 #3. Text by Dober Spalding. Medium B3-D5/C♯4-C♯5. *E.* Diatonic with simple melodic patterns. Several meter changes from 6/8 to 9/8, yet rhythms remain quite accessible. Guitar part consists primarily of straightforward chordal accompaniment figures.

340 Marina, Carmen. *Three Songs* (Spanish). 197-/c1983 Library of Congress. Text by various authors. Medium A3-A5/D4-C5. *M.* Group of three diverse songs (6'). Diatonic, stepwise melodies with strong Spanish musical influences. Rhythms are varied yet not complicated. Guitar is rather prominent in song #1; however, in the others it essentially plays repetitive accompaniment figures.

341 Martinsson, Rolf. *Poemes Japonais* (Swedish). 1985/c1985 Guilys. High G3-A5/A3-F5. *VD.* Unconventional, improvisatory structure for both voice and guitar. Demanding vocal part calls for wide leaps and sustained high notes, in addition to some narrated lines and sections of improvisation based on specified sets of pitches.

342 Marttinen, Tauno. *Espanjalainen Rapsodia* (Finnish). 1989/c1989 Finland 10102,3,4,5. Text by Elisabet Larila. High or Medium B3-G5/B3-E4. *M.* Group of four songs (14'). Tonal with mostly traditional harmonies and accessible vocal lines in various tempi, moods, and difficulty levels. Song #4 features rapid melismas and is unmetered (as is song #1), yet rhythms are not complicated. Accessible, accompanimental guitar.

343 Marttinen, Tauno. *Seitsemän Kansanlaulua Kitaran Säestyksellä* (Finnish). 1977 Finland 79871. High or Medium A3-E5/C4-D5. *E.* Group of seven mostly strophic songs (14'). Tonal with traditional harmonies. Simple, straightforward melodies and basic rhythms. Contrasting tempi between pieces. Song #5 provides an alternate, more active accompaniment. Guitar largely outlines chords in diverse, often animated ways.

344 Mather, Bruce. *Cycle Rilke* (German). 1960/c1972 Canada MV 1102 M427cy. Text by Rainer Maria Rilke. Tenor B2-A4/D3-A♭4. *VD*. Cycle of three songs (9'). Atonal with frequent dissonances. Much disjunct, chromatic melodic motion. Constantly changing meters. Extended vocal lines with many long, sustained tones at varying dynamic levels. Highly challenging, independent guitar part.

345 Maw, Nicholas. *Six Interiors* (English). 1966/c1977 Boosey 20354. Text by Thomas Hardy from *Collected Poems of Thomas Hardy*. High G3-A♭5/E♭4-F♯5. *VD*. Group of six songs (18'). Highly chromatic with elusive tonality. Melodic motion ranges from stepwise chromaticism to wide leaps exceeding an octave. Meter changes provide rhythm challenges. Widely varied moods, due to text and expressive, complex guitar part.

346 Medek, Tilo. *Fensterscheiben* (German). 1969/c1971 Neue NM 285. Text by Jens Gerlach. Tenor F♯3-F♯4/A3-F♯4. *E*. From the 12-song collection ...*und die Liebe braucht ein Dach*, compiled by Helge Jung and Werner Pauli. Simple diatonic melody, the bulk of which alternates between A3 and B3 with variations in rhythm. Guitar part consists of a simple, repeated pattern.

347 Medek, Tilo. *Das Lied von der Wolke der Nacht* (German). 1968/c1971 Neue NM 285. Text by Bertolt Brecht. Tenor D3-G4/F♯3-E4. *M*. From the 12-song collection ...*und die Liebe braucht ein Dach*, compiled by Helge Jung and Werner Pauli. Mostly diatonic melody accompanied by somewhat dissonant, nonfunctional harmonies. Brief sections of duple vs. triple meter. Simple guitar part.

348 Medek, Tilo. *Vor dem Küssen* (German). 1967/c1971 Neue NM 285. Text by Georg Maurer. Tenor E3-E4/G3-D4. *M*. From the 12-song collection ...*und die Liebe braucht ein Dach*, compiled by Helge Jung and Werner Pauli. Diatonic melody with varying rhythm patterns and changing meters. Simple chordal guitar accompaniment.

349 Meijering, Cord. *November* (German). 1988/c1988 Moeck 5382. Text by Peter Steffens. Soprano or Mezzo G♯3-F♯5/B3-F♯5. *VD*. Atonal with wide, often unusual chromatic intervals and numerous changes into irregular meters. Guitar part has complex rhythms and utilizes uncommon percussive sound effects.

350 Meyers, Randall. *Zen Songs* (English). 1983 Norway S 400 MEY. Text by various Japanese authors. Soprano B♭3-B♭5/E4-F♯5. *D*. Group of six songs (14'). Tonal, with mostly diatonic, legato phrases and uncomplicated rhythms. Moods are varied yet subdued. Song #3 has several long, chromatic melismas, and a glissando from B♭5 to B♭3 followed by burping. Guitar is very expressive and varied, with unconventional timbres.

351 Migot, Georges. *Trois Chants de Joie et de Soucis* (French). c1980 Trans EMT 1539. Text by Pierre Moussarie. High D4-G5/D4-E5. *M.* Group of three songs (7'). Diatonic, lyric vocal lines with uncomplicated rhythms. Varied in tempo and mood as indicated by the work's title. Diverse and active guitar part.

352 Mittergradnegger, Günther. *Heiteres Herbarium* (German). 1959/c1968 Doblinger GKM 78. Text by Karl Heinrich Waggerl. High A♯3-A5/G4-G5. *D.* Cycle of 10 short songs (10'). Chromatic tonality with occasional dissonances. Mostly stepwise and simple disjunct melodic motion. Simple rhythms despite some meter changes. Some spoken sections. Varied tempi and moods. Substantial yet accessible guitar part.

353 Mittergradnegger, Günther. *Ich Hab Dir ein Lied Gesponnen* (German). 1988/c1993 Doblinger GKM 173. Text by various authors. High B3-A5/A4-F♯5. *D.* Cycle of six short songs (8') set to text of African origin. Mostly diatonic, yet has numerous dissonances between the voice and guitar. Uncomplicated rhythms despite frequent meter changes. Some spoken and declamatory sections. Varied, active guitar part.

354 Morales, Carlos Ovidio. *Canción de Cuna* (Spanish). 1985/c1986 Puerto Rico. Text by Angeles Pastor. High C4-G5/G4-G5. *E.* From the collection *La Cancion de Arte en Puerto Rico.* Diatonic with simple, repetitive melody. Easy guitar accompaniment, consisting solely of one block chord per measure.

355 Morales Giácoman, Luis. *Canciones del Poeta Místico* (Spanish). 1989 composer. Text by Fernando Rielo Pardal from *Dios y árbol* and *Balcón a la Bahía.* Soprano C♯4-G5/F♯4-E5. *D.* Cycle of four songs (12'). Tonal with some chromaticism. Mostly stepwise melodic motion. Rhythms can be difficult due to irregularly changing meters. Some rapid fioraturi typical of Spanish music. Guitar features repeated accompanimental patterns.

356 Morales Giácoman, Luis. *Cuánto Fin en Instantes que Se Amar* (Spanish). 1991 composer. Text by Fernando Rielo Pardal from *Balcón a la Bahía.* Soprano C♯4-G5/F♯4-E5. *D.* Tonal with much chromaticism. Well-balanced mix of conjunct and disjunct melodic motion. Long, lento vocal phrases utilizing varied rhythm patterns. Several unaccompanied ad libitum vocal passages. Prominent, independent guitar has solo introduction.

357 Morales Giácoman, Luis. *Dolor Entre Cristales (Tríptico #1)* (Spanish). 1991 composer. Text by Fernando Rielo Pardal from *Dolor Entre Cristales.*

Soprano D4-B5/E4-F5. *D*. Cycle of three songs (7'). Tonal with some chromaticism. Mixed melodic motion incorporating some rapid fioratura and melismas. Rhythms are not difficult except in song #3, due to its constant, unmarked changing of unusual meters. Cycle ends on glissando up to B5.

358 Morales Giácoman, Luis. *Dolor Entre Cristales (Tríptico #2)* (Spanish). 1993 composer. Text by Fernando Rielo Pardal from *Dolor Entre Cristales*. Soprano B3-G#5/E4-F#5. *D*. Cycle of three songs (8'). Tonal with some chromaticism. Accessible melodies utilizing both stepwise and disjunct motion. Some meter changes, especially in song #3 making for unusual rhythms there. Active guitar part contains sectionalized repeated patterns.

359 Morales Giácoman, Luis. *Enterraste Mis Besos* (Spanish). 1989 composer. Text by Fernando Rielo Pardal from *Dios y árbol*. Soprano D4-G5/F4-E5. *D*. Tonal with some chromaticism. Features mostly stepwise melodic motion. Several sectional meter changes and little rhythm pattern repetition. Modern yet consonant harmonies, with voice pitch often not repeated in guitar. Tranquil yet active guitar is not difficult.

360 Morales Giácoman, Luis. *Magdalena y el Amor* (Spanish). 1993 composer. Text by Magdelena Lasala from *Seré Leve y Paracerá que No Te Amo*. Soprano D4-G#5/E4-E5. *D*. Cycle of five songs (10'). Accessible, chromatic melodies with a Spanish flavor accompanied by contemporary, sometimes dissonant harmonies in an overall tonal setting. A wide variety of moods and tempi. Many meter changes. Active, substantial guitar part.

361 Morales Giácoman, Luis. *Marchemos a la Era* (Spanish). 1990 composer. Text by Fernando Rielo Pardal from *Balcón a la Bahía*. Soprano D#4-F#5/F#4-D#5. *D*. Chromatic, sometimes difficult legato melodies sung over an often dissonant, repetitious chordal guitar pattern. Tonally elusive. Several sections feature an ametrical vocalise with improvisatory guitar. Difficulty lies more in ensemble than in separate parts.

362 Morales Giácoman, Luis. *Nueva York, Sepultada por la Lluvia* (Spanish). 1991 composer. Text by Fernando Rielo Pardal from *Dolor Entre Cristales*. Soprano E4-G#5/F#4-F#5. *D*. Diatonic with mostly stepwise melodic motion and straightforward rhythms. However, the vocal pitch is frequently dissonant with the guitar. Several meter changes. Rapid guitar pattern similar to broken chords is repeated throughout entire piece.

363 Moreno, Ismael. *Nunca Como Mi Querer* (Spanish). c1967 Ricordi S.A. BA12630. Low A3-C4/A3-C4. *E*. Diatonic with simple, repetitious, disjunct melodies in strophic form. Guitar has a fairly rapid solo introduction, but as soon as the vocal melody begins it features a straightforward broken chord accompaniment that is not difficult.

364 Moreno-Torroba, Federico. *Como Quieres Que Te De* (Spanish). c1970 Dim. Text by composer. Medium D4-F#5/E4-E5. *M.* Mostly diatonic, featuring many elements associated with Spanish folk music, such as melodic ornamentations and some florid, melismatic passages. Guitar part is essentially accompanimental, consisting largely of arpeggio and chordal patterns.

365 Moss, Piotr. *Dédicace III* (Polish). 1995 composer. Soprano C#4-A5/E4-F5. *D.* Atonal, with expressive vocal line often supported harmonically by guitar. Some difficult intervals amidst generally smooth but fragmented vocal phrases. Intricate rhythms with almost constant meter changes in an adagio tempo. A wide, flexible dynamic range is required, most notably in the upper pitches. Challenging, somewhat sparse guitar part.

366 Mostad, Jon. *Fråga och Svar* (Swedish). 1980 Norway S 400 MOS. Text by various authors. Tenor C3-A#4/D3-E4. *VD.* Group of two atonal songs (14'); #2 consists of three songs within. #1 alternates brief, sequential melodies and spoken phrases, then ends with humming. The songs in #2 musically vary; the first two are more conventional, while the last is ametrical. Challenging, very significant guitar part.

367 Müller, Siegfried. *Fünf Chansons* (German). c1977 Neue NM 354. Text by various authors. Medium A3-Eb5/E4-D5. *M.* Group of five songs (10'). Mostly diatonic with generally accessible, mixed melodic motion. Simple, often repetitive rhythms. Song #5 features a recitative-like introduction and portamenti. Varied in mood and tempi. Uncomplicated guitar part often accompanimental.

368 Müller-Hornbach, Gerhard. *5 Gesänge der Schirin.* 1983/c1983 Breitkopf EB 9004. Soprano C#4-Bb5/F4-G5. *VD.* Cycle of five songs (10'). Serial in design, featuring repetitious pitch and interval sequences. Rhythms are ametrical and mostly notated in approximate durations. Vocal sounds consist of repeated phonetic sounds. Many detailed, unusual guitar sounds are specified.

369 Musgrave, Thea. *Five Love Songs* (English). 1955/c1970 Chester JWC 454. Text by various 16th- and 17th-century authors. Soprano C4-A5/E4-F#5. *D.* Group of five songs (10'). Tonally elusive, with much chromaticism. Each song differs greatly in terms of technical difficulty and musical affection. Long, sustained vocal lines are very common. The second song features rapid melismas. Varied, active guitar part.

370 Musgrave, Thea. *Sir Patrick Spens* (English). 1961/c1976 Chester JWC 55066. Tenor Bb2-A4/D3-G#4. *VD.* (7'). Atonal with often difficult disjunct melodic motion. Frequent meter changes and intricate rhythms. Story of a seafaring sailor set in Old English. Incorporates a wide range of dynamics and is quite dramatic at times. Complex, autonomous guitar part.

371 Nielsen, Tage. *Five Romantic Songs* (English). 1994/c1994 Samfundet. Text by various authors. Mezzo E4-F5/F4-F5. *D.* Group of five songs (12'). Cadential chords and lyrical melodies in narrow tessitura often imply tonal center, but frequent dissonances make tonality elusive and vocal lines challenging. Unusual meters in song #2; accessible rhythms elsewhere in varied, relaxed tempi. Guitar is often melodic in design.

372 Nieminen, Kai. *Sea Poems and a Postludium* (Finnish). 1979/c1979 Finland 6649. Medium Bb3-Eb5/D4-B4. *D.* Atonal, with chromatic vocal lines of disjunct motion that are often strongly supported in the guitar. Repeated notes and short rhythms in long phrases combined with many meter changes in slow tempi yield effect of speech. Fragmented guitar is often tacet during the song, but has a substantial solo postludium.

373 Nightingale, Daniel. *Appalachian Triptych* (English). c1993 composer. Text from Appalachian folk songs. Medium A3-F5/D4-D5. *M.* Cycle of three songs (8') based on well-known American folk tunes. Song #2 utilizes some hand clapping and concludes with a challenging guitar accelerando. Song #3 features a long section of humming and requires guitarist to play with flesh of fingers.

374 Nightingale, Daniel. *War Cries* (English). 1990/c1990 Acoma, also AMC M1624 N688 W2. Text by various authors. Soprano or Mezzo Ab3-A5/C4-D5. *D.* Cycle of two songs (8'35"). Chromatic, with an elusive tonality. Varied rhythms and frequent meter changes. Much disjunct melodic motion in first song, yet intervals rarely exceed M6. Very challenging guitar utilizes many timbres, especially in song #2.

375 Nix, Michael. *Three American Folk Songs* (English). 1983/c1984 AMC M1624 N7358 A5. Medium B3-E5/B3-C5. *E.* Group of three songs (8'). Traditional folk melodies with new and varied accompaniments specifically written for classical guitar.

376 Nørgaard, Helmer. *13 Prosodier* (Danish). 1990 composer. Text from ancient Chinese poems. Mezzo C4-A5/E4-F5. *D.* Group of 13 songs (24'). Tonally elusive and varied in its use of melodic motion, dissonance, meter, tempo, rhythms, and mood. Unconventional techniques include speaking, glissandi, quasi-improvisation and various guitar effects. Sparse texture due to guitar's frequent lack of chords.

377 Nørgård, Per. *Freedom* (English). 1977/c1977 Hansen. Text by Walt Whitman from *Seadrift*. Medium Bb3-D5/B3-Db5. *D.* Tonal with chromaticism and mixed melodic motion. Some complex rhythms due to unusual meter changes. Guitar part is based on a simple three-chord motive which becomes progressively more embellished and complex.

378 Nørgård, Per. *Libra (1973)* (German). 1973/c1976 Hansen WH 29320 A. Text by Rudolf Steiner. Tenor C#3-D5/E3-G4. *VD*. Cycle of three songs (13'), the first and third consisting of solo guitar. Highly chromatic with some very disjunct melodic motion and complex rhythms, yet somewhat lyric in design. Requires forte sustained high notes and falsetto. Very demanding guitar part.

379 Nørholm, Ib. *Blomster fra den Danske Poesis Flora* (Danish). 1987/c1987 Engstrøm E&S 562. Text by various authors. High B3-G5/E4-E5. *D*. Group of eight strophic songs (15'), some quite brief. Very diverse difficulty levels due to widely changing degrees of tonality, dissonance, melodic motion, and meter for each song. Slow tempi and terse vocal rhythms predominate. Harmonically interesting, sometimes challenging guitar.

380 Nørholm, Ib. *Tavole per Orfeo* (Danish). 1967/c1974 Hansen WH 29139. Text by Poul Borum. Mezzo A3-G#5/B3-E♭5. *VD*. Cycle of six pieces (22'); three songs are alternated with three guitar solos. Songs #1 and #5 feature chromatic, disjunct lyricism and many meter changes. Song #3 requires extended vocal techniques and the use of a cigarette and unconventional instruments (glass chimes and thundersheet).

381 Nørholm, Ib. *Whispers of Heavenly Death* (English). 1987/c1992 Kontrapunkt EK 1019. Text by Walt Whitman. Soprano D4-A♭5/E♭4-F5. *VD*. Atonal, with disjunct, sometimes fragmented chromatic vocal lines that are often dissonant to the guitar. Diverse yet uncomplicated meters and rhythms in a slow tempo (M.M. 56). Challenging guitar part is varied and quite active, with harmonics and unusual rhythms.

382 Norton, David D. *Break, Break, Break* (English). 1992 composer. Text by Alfred, Lord Tennyson. Medium or Low B3-B4/D4-A4. *E*. Diatonic, featuring sectional shifts of minor and major. ABA form with mostly stepwise melodic motion and simple, repetitive rhythms in an allegro 3/8. The text is a lament for a lost loved one. Quite accessible guitar part consists almost entirely of arpeggiated sixteenth-note chords.

383 Norton, David D. *The Owl & the Pussycat* (English). 1996 composer. Text by Edward Lear. Medium B3-D#5/D#4-C#5. *E*. Diatonic strophic song, described by the composer as being in a "quasi-Victorian parlor style," in which the performers should provide some "'over the top' schmalzing." Simple melody and repetitive, accessible guitar help to keep the light, humorous text in the forefront.

384 Novák, Jan. *Apicius Modulatus* (Latin). c1971 Zanibon G. 5146 Z. High D4-B5/A4-A5. *VD*. Cycle of nine songs (17'), of which the first and last are for solo guitar. Somewhat chromatic and tonally elusive. Mostly disjunct, angular melodic motion. Many unmarked changes to unusual meters. Text deals with basic rules of culinary art. Demanding guitar.

385 Novák, Jan. *Cantiones Latinae* (Latin). c1972 Zanibon G. 5259 Z. Text by various authors. Medium C4-F#5/E4-D5. *M.* Group of 14 strophic songs (30') based on Latin songs mostly from the Middle Ages and Renaissance. Diatonic with simple rhythms and accessible melodic motion. Guitar is rather active and moderately challenging, yet essentially accompanimental in nature.

386 Nunes, Rhonda Lynne. *Romancero Gitano* (Spanish). 1985/c1985 AMC M1624 N972 R7 2. Text by Federico García Lorca. Female B3-C6/ C3-G5. *D.* Cycle of three songs (6'24") with a distinctive Spanish flavor. Vocal part contains leaps requiring great agility. Utilizes numerous meter changes. Active guitar part is predominantly chordal, yet its texture varies often.

387 Olcott-Bickford, Vahdah. *Nectar* (English). *Guitar Review* #24. Text by composer. Medium E4-C#5/E4-C#5. *E.* Short song (30") consisting of a very simple, pastoral melody over an accessibly fast and repetitious guitar accompaniment.

388 O'Leary, Martin. *Three Lyrics* (English). 1987 Ireland. Text by James Joyce from *Chamber Music*. Mezzo G3-B4/B3-B4. *D.* Cycle of three songs (10'). Atonal with relatively smooth, chromatic melodic motion. Consistently introspective mood. Song #1 is ametrical, featuring alternating solo passages between the voice and guitar. Meters, often unusual, change constantly in songs #2 & 3, yet rhythms are not too difficult.

389 Orr, Buxton. *Ballad of Mr. and Mrs. Discobbolos* (English). 1965/c1994 Gamber. Text by Edward Lear. Tenor C#3-A4/D3-E4. *D.* (10'). May also be performed by two voices: one male, one female. Chromatic with much dissonance. Mixed melodic motion with uncomplicated, often repetitive rhythms in a lively 6/8 setting. Light-hearted text. Active, varied and challenging guitar part.

390 Orrego-Salas, Juan. *Canciones en el Estilo Popular* (Spanish). 1981/c1981 MMB X815001. Text by Pablo Neruda from *Odes Elementales*. High C4-A5/E4-F5. *D.* Group of three strophic songs (9') with a distinctly Spanish flavor. Tonal with chromatic, colorful guitar harmonies which are often somewhat dissonant to the voice. Largely stepwise melodic motion and simple rhythms. Active, accessible guitar accompaniment.

391 Ortiz, William. *A Delicate Fire* (English). 1986/c1986 composer, also AMC. Text by Olga Mendell. Alto F#3-E5/A3-B4. *D.* Cycle of three songs (18'). Mostly diatonic, yet song #2 features numerous dissonances between voice and guitar. Largely stepwise melodic motion. Uncomplicated, often repetitious rhythms with slow tempi. Quiet, meditative mood maintained throughout cycle.

392 Ortiz, William. *La Mano de Hielo* (Spanish). 1978/c1978 composer. Text by Hugo Margenat. Alto G3-E5/B3-D5. *VD*. Atonal with much dissonance between voice and guitar. Mostly disjunct melodic motion, yet intervals rarely exceed M6. Complex rhythms with numerous meter and tempo changes. Wide range of dynamics and moods. Challenging, constantly varying guitar part.

393 Ortiz, William. *Romance* (Spanish). 1988/c1988 composer. Text by Carlos Varo. Soprano/Boy Soprano E4-F5/E4-E5. *E*. Diatonic with simple mixed melodic motion. Highly accessible, repetitive rhythms in a slow 6/8 setting. Long vocal phrases. Active, uncomplicated guitar part features several prolonged solo passages, most notably at the beginning and end of piece.

394 Ourkouzounov, Atanas. *Trois Chansons* (Bulgarian). 1994/c1994 composer. Mezzo D4-A5/F4-E5. *D*. Group of three songs (10'). Tonal with chromaticism. Accessible melodic motion, with uncomplicated rhythms in songs #1 and #3. The second song is in 9/16, and contains dissonances near its end atypical of the rest of the work. Active, repetitive guitar part.

395 Pakker, Henk. *Towards Anthony Holborne* (English). 1981 Donemus. Text by various authors. Any voice range. *D*. Cycle of seven songs (14') for reciter and guitar. The optional texts are spoken before each guitar piece, and consist of poems by William Shakespeare (#7) and Barbara S. Worembrand (#1-6). Guitar part is mostly atonal and often challenging, revealing a diverse array of moods and tempi.

396 Paraskevas, Apostolos. *Stopping by Woods...* (English). 1995 composer. Text by Robert Frost from *Stopping by Woods on a Snowy Evening*. Soprano D4-G5/F#4-D5. *D*. Atonal, with chromatic, relatively smooth melodic motion and accessible rhythms. Many legato, tranquil vocal lines in a moderato tempo are contrasted by a recurring faster section that is more agitated. Substantial guitar is often accompanimental, yet has several expressive solo passages.

397 Parris, Robert. *Cynthia's Revells* (English). 1979/c1979 composer, also ACA 14144. Text by Ben Jonson. Baritone F♭2-E4/F#2-C#4. *VD*. Cycle of three songs (7'). Atonal with highly disjunct, chromatic melodic motion; vocal leaps are frequently in excess of P8. First two songs are rhythmically challenging due to constant meter changes, while the third is ametrical. Sparse, independent guitar part.

398 Pauli, Werner. *Genosse Feherlei* (German). c1980 Neue NM 430. Text by Johannes Robert Becher. Tenor G3-G4/G3-D4. *E*. From the 11-song collection *Ich Liebe Dich*, compiled by Sonja Kehler. Very short song (45"). Tonal with simple, mostly stepwise melody set almost entirely in eighth-note rhythms, yielding a light-hearted effect. Simple yet effective guitar accompaniment. See entry #402.

399 Pauli, Werner. *Ich Liebe Dich* (German). c1980 Neue NM 430. Text by Johannes Robert Becher. Tenor E3-A4/A3-F#4. *D*. From the 11-song collection *Ich Liebe Dich*, compiled by Sonja Kehler. Tonal with some chromaticism, mostly in the guitar. Melody is varied by sections of original pitches contrasted with new disjunct phrases. Much rhythmic repetition.

400 Pauli, Werner. *Der Rederfluß* (German). c1980 Neue NM 430. Text by Johannes Robert Becher. Tenor A♭3-A♭4/D4-G4. *M*. From the 11-song collection *Ich Liebe Dich*, compiled by Sonja Kehler. Tonal with some chromaticism, featuring somewhat disjunct melodic motion. Simple eighth-note rhythms throughout, yet guitar often has triplets. Strophic in form, with a brief coda.

401 Pauli, Werner. *Still, Mein Herz* (German). c1980 Neue NM 430. Text by Johannes Robert Becher. Tenor E3-G4/F3-E4. *E*. From the 11-song collection *Ich Liebe Dich*, compiled by Sonja Kehler. Diatonic with simple rhythms in 6/8 meter. Some disjunct motion, with intervals of M6 and M7. Verses 1, 2 and 4 share the same melody. Guitar part is texturally sparse and uncomplicated.

402 Pauli, Werner. *Über Selbstkritik* (German). c1980 Neue NM 430. Text by Johannes Robert Becher. Tenor G3-G4/G3-D4. *E*. From the 11-song collection *Ich Liebe Dich*, compiled by Sonja Kehler. Very short song (45"). Same melody as Pauli's *Genosse Fehlerlei* (see entry #398); the guitar part is slightly different and more repetitive. It appears that the two songs should be performed together.

403 Pauli, Werner. *Das Wunder* (German). c1980 Neue NM 430. Text by Johannes Robert Becher. Tenor C3-F#4/G3-D4. *E*. From the 11-song collection *Ich Liebe Dich*, compiled by Sonja Kehler. Mostly diatonic with stepwise melodic motion and simple rhythms. Very accessible guitar part, yet its accompanimental patterns constantly vary.

404 Pelletier, Marie. *Duo No. 6.* 1991 composer, also Canada MV1102P388du048. Soprano A3-D6/D4-A5. *VD*. Tonality is emphasized via constantly repeated pitches instead of functional harmony. Phonetic sounds set to fragmented, disjunct melodic motion. Widely varied, sometimes complex rhythm patterns. Uses effects such as glissando, nasality, and percussive guitar.

405 Pennisi, Francesco. *Al Precario Sentiero* (Italian). 1990/c1990 Ricordi 135475. Text by composer. Soprano F#4-A5/F#4-F#5. *VD*. Atonal with mixed, highly chromatic melodic motion. Diverse, complex rhythms in both parts which are often oppositional. The intricate dynamics vary frequently and rarely exceed mezzo forte. Several difficult, rapid melismas. Guitar has various ametrical solos.

406 Pinkham, Daniel. *Antiphons* (Latin). c1987 Ione ECS 4169. Text by Gregory from *Liber Responsalis*. Medium B3-F#5/E4-E5. *D*. Cycle of seven songs (7'30"). Contemporary settings of medieval chant texts. Atonal in nature, with much chromaticism and dissonance between voice and guitar. Frequent meter changes and constantly varied, often asymmetrical rhythms. Guitar part texturally sparse.

407 Pinkham, Daniel. *Charm Me Asleep* (English). c1978 Ione ECS 169. Words from Old English texts. Medium A3-F#5/C4-E5. *D*. Cycle of 10 songs (19'), the first being for solo guitar. Tonally chromatic with accessible, mixed melodic motion. Rhythms are not difficult except in songs #7 and #8, which are somewhat challenging. Quite varied in mood and tempi. Varied, stimulating guitar part.

408 Pinkham, Daniel. *In Youth Is Pleasure* (English). c1974 Schirmer ECS 2814. Text by Robert Wever. Medium A3-D5/B3-B4. *M*. Tonal with some chromaticism. Features simple rhythms and mixed, accessible melodic motion in a moderato setting. Very lyric, with long, connected vocal phrases. Uncomplicated guitar is often repetitive, and accompanimental in nature.

409 Pinkham, Daniel. *The Lamb* (English). c1970 Ione ECS Choral 2594. Text by William Blake. High D4-G5/E4-E5. *E*. Mostly diatonic with straightforward, repetitive rhythm and melodic patterns in an andante setting. Text is of a religious nature. Simple guitar accompaniment, consisting mostly of sustained single tones and chords.

410 Pinkham, Daniel. *Man, That Is Born of a Woman* (English). c1971 Schirmer ECS 143. Text from *Book of Common Prayer*. Mezzo F#3-F5/Ab3-D5. *VD*. Cycle of three songs (8'). Atonal with much disjunct melodic motion, notably in first song, with intervals often exceeding an octave. Many meter changes. Generally slow tempi throughout. Often dissonant between voice and mostly single-note guitar, which may be electric.

411 Pinkham, Daniel. *O Wholesome Night* (English). 1982/c1982 Ione ECS 174. Text by Norma Farber. Medium A3-Eb5/B3-C5. *D*. Tonally elusive, with little functional harmony and much dissonant chromaticism. Mostly stepwise melodic motion in a lyric moderato setting. Vocal part features uncomplicated 2/4 rhythms that often contrast with the guitar's almost constant single eighth-note 6/8 patterns.

412 Plá Sales, Roberto. *Cuatro Canciones Sefardíes* (Spanish). c1965 Union UME 20777. Text by composer. Medium C#4-F#5/E4-E5. *D*. Group of four strophic songs (12') utilizing elements of traditional Spanish folk music. Features much challenging vocal ornamentation. Predominantly slow tempi throughout. Active and varied guitar part is not difficult.

413 Platts, Kenneth. *Four Poems of Robert Graves* (English). c1980 Ashdown E.A. 37757. Text by Robert Graves. High B3-A♭5/E4-F5. *D.* Group of four songs (10'). Tonal with chromaticism, featuring long, lyric vocal passages with much disjunct melodic motion and accessible rhythms. Marked contrast between each piece in terms of tempo and mood. Guitar accompaniment is quite varied.

414 Polin, Claire. *Wind Songs* (several languages). 1978 composer, also Aureus. Text by various authors. Soprano G♭3-A5/C4-E5. *VD.* Cycle of two songs (11'). Atonal with much disjunct melodic motion and dissonance. Intricate, demanding rhythms. The two songs are respectively in Welsh and Russian with an English version added. Various unconventional techniques employed. Often very dramatic.

415 Potter, Rick. *Guitar Songs, Volume 1* (English). 1986/c1986 Scotland. Text by various authors. Soprano B3-B5/F4-A5. *VD.* Group of four songs (7'). Atonal and often dissonant. Songs #1 and #4 are very chromatic and rhythmically complex, with the latter also being quite disjunct melodically. Song #1 has B5-B3 glissando. The other two songs are less demanding. Repetitive guitar part.

416 Potter, Rick. *Guitar Songs, Volume 2* (English). 1993/c1993 Scotland. Text by various authors. Soprano D4-B5/E4-F♯5. *VD.* Group of four songs (9'). Chromatic, mixed melodic motion with most intervals smaller than P5. Guitar often implies a tonal center, yet the voice is usually dissonant to it. Some unusual rhythm subdivisions. Many long, legato phrases. Active, varied guitar.

417 Prosperi, Carlo. *Tre Frammenti di Saffo* (Italian). 1983/c1983 Zerboni S. 9263 Z. Text by Sappho. Soprano C♯4-A5/F♯4-F♯5. *D.* Group of three songs (6'). Ambiguous tonality, with long, legato chromatic vocal phrases of somewhat smooth melodic motion. Rhythms are not complicated. Second song requires sustained fortissimo high notes (G♭5-A5). Last song uses motives from first song. Accessible guitar crucial in varying mood.

418 Raditschnig, Werner. *Chansongs* (German). 1986 composer. Text by Reinhold Aumaier. Medium A3-D5/C♯4-C♯5. *D.* Group of three songs (6'). Varied in compositional style; song #1 is based on traditional harmonic schemes, while the other two are atonal, with frequent dissonances between guitar and voice. An "actor/singer" suggested, most likely due to speech-like fragmented vocal lines and sprechstimme.

419 Raditschnig, Werner. *Drei Hörbilder* (German). 1986 composer. Text by Reinhold Aumaier. Any voice range. *D.* Group of three songs (5'). "Actor/

singer" suggested; vocalist's past consists solely of spoken phrases, with no singing. Atonal and ametrical, with an improvisatory atmosphere. Active, challenging guitar.

420 Raditschnig, Werner. *Flucht vor Algol* (German). 1983 composer. Any voice range. *D.* (50'). Highly improvisatory; the score is comprised solely of isolated pictorial and atonal musical fragments. Vocal part consists entirely of spoken phrases, with no singing; acting out "scenes" (of one's own design) encouraged. Many nontraditional techniques are featured and suggested.

421 Raditschnig, Werner. *Gottlieder* (German). 1986 composer. Text by Reinhold Aumaier. Baritone F2-A4/B2-B3. *VD.* (8'). Atonal and mostly ametrical, utilizing much improvisation. Vocal part has very wide pitch range, with chromatic lines containing few large leaps. Rhythms are accessible. Some nontraditional techniques are featured. Guitarist plays solely via glass slides in both hands.

422 Raditschnig, Werner. *Notturno.* 1988 composer. Alto E3-F#5/G3-D5. *VD.* (8'). Highly improvisatory; the score is comprised solely of isolated pictorial and atonal musical fragments requiring many nontraditional techniques. Vocal part consists entirely of phonetic sounds mimicking Korean. Guitar requires special tuning associated with Korean instruments.

423 Raheb, Jeff. *En Mi Cielo al Crepescular* (Spanish). Composer, also AMC M1624 R147 E5. Text by Pablo Neruda. Soprano A3-Ab5/E4-E5. *M.* Tonal with some chromaticism. Mixed, accessible melodic motion and uncomplicated rhythms despite meter changes. Melodic design, use of ornamentation and mild dissonances yield a Spanish flavor. Active, primarily accompanimental guitar is not difficult.

424 Raheb, Jeff. *Juegas Todos los Dias* (Spanish). 1981/c1981 composer, also AMC M1624 R147 J9. Text by Pablo Neruda. High E4-C6/E4-E5. *D.* Tonal with chromaticism, often yielding colorful, dissonant harmonies frequently associated with Spanish music. Mixed, chromatic melodic motion with varied rhythms and unusual meters. Uncharacteristically high tessitura in last nine measures.

425 Rainier, Priaulx. *Dance of the Rain* (English). 1947/c1968 Schott ED 11064. Text from Afrikaans of Eugene Marais. High D4-G5/G4-E5. *D.* Diatonic, with rapid, speech-like phrases of often stagnant melodic motion mimicking African chant music in its rhythmic variety and complexity. Very brisk and energetic, aided by the challenging guitar part's constant forward momentum. Although there are some contrasting soft sections, the bulk of the piece requires powerful, vigorous singing.

426 Rainier, Priaulx. *Ubunzima (Misfortune)* (Zulu). 1948/c1968 Schott ED 11064. High Eb4-Bb5/Gb4-Db5. *D.* Quasi-modal, featuring somber yet agitated exclamatory phrases mimicking Zulu cries, with complex rhythms in 10/8 meter. The guitar part consists almost exclusively of rhythmically repetitive (mostly eighth-note), stepwise second inversion chords, often dissonant to the vocal line.

427 Rasmussen, Karl Aage. *When I Was Happy I Wrote No Songs* (Swedish). 1967/c1977 Hansen WH 29388. Text from gypsy songs. Baritone F2-F#4/Bb2-D4. *VD.* (14'10"). Described as "seven lyrical improvisations." Atonal and ametrical. Unconventional techniques such as speaking, glissando, whispering and relative pitch levels. English singing version is given. Difficult guitar part is quite fragmented at times.

428 Rechberger, Herman. *Canciónes* (Spanish). 1989/c1989 Finland 9888. Text by Federico García Lorca. High E3-Bb5/F3-F#5. *VD.* Cycle of five songs (10'), of which #1 & 5 are identical and virtually a cappella. Atonal chromatic vocal lines are often disjunct, with mostly accessible rhythms. Varying tessitura; song #2 has a very wide range (E3-A5), and song #4 lies mostly around E5-G#5. Diverse mood and tempi. Guitar part is often very dissonant yet not too difficult, due to its repetitiveness.

429 Reid, Clement. *Three Greek Songs* (English). 1982/c1996 CNY. Text by various authors from *Greek Poetry for Everyman.* Medium G#3-C#5/C#4-B4. *D.* Group of three songs (10'). Much dissonance between guitar and voice, yet sense of tonality exists due to repetitive parts for both performers. Relatively smooth melodic motion. Varied tempi, intricate rhythmic subdivisions, and unusual meters. Consistently soft dynamic levels throughout contribute to an overall subdued mood.

430 Richter Herf, Franz. *Vom Leben das Beste* (German). 1986 Helbling. Text by Paula Grogger. Medium or Low B3-C#5/C#4-B5. *VD.* The primary challenge in this atonal work lies in its unique tuning system, where certain pitches for both players are slightly higher or lower than in conventional equal temperament (precise indications provided). The only other significant challenge is the dissonance between the voice and guitar, the latter of which is mostly chordal in design.

431 Riou, Alain Michel. *Poésie Primitive.* 1991 composer. Mezzo A3-F#5/D4-F5. *VD.* Atonal, with many long, legato vocal lines of chromatic melodic motion that is not excessively disjunct. Text consists of French phonetic sounds. Challenging rhythms amidst frequent meter and tempo changes. Difficult, often texturally sparse guitar works independently of the voice.

432 Riou, Alain Michel. *Un Silence* (French). 1992 composer. Text by Jacques Roubard from *Dors.* Mezzo G3-G5/B3-F5. *VD.* Described by composer as a vocalise. Atonal, with highly disjunct chromatic melodic motion in long phrases. Complex rhythms and changing meters in various slow tempi.

Voice part combines poem text with French phonetic sounds. Difficult, sometimes sparse guitar part may be played on piano or omitted.

433 Ritchie, John. *Five William Blake Songs of Innocence* (English). 1994/c1994 composer, also Sounz. Text by William Blake. High D4-A5/E4-F5. *D.* Group of five songs (12'45"). Tonal with some chromaticism, in mostly lighthearted, relaxed settings. Many long, legato vocal phrases. Widely diverse yet accessible melodic motion and straightforward rhythms. Song #3 features frequent meter changes. Active, prominent guitar is not complicated.

434 Robinovitch, Sid. *Canciones Sefardies* (Spanish). 1978/c1978 Canada MV 1102 R656ca. Text from *Chants Judéo-Espagnols.* Medium B♭3-G5/D4-E5. *VD.* Group of five songs (15'). Based on folk texts of the Sephardic Jews of Turkey, utilizing a distinctive Judeo-Spanish dialect. The songs have a strong Spanish flavor, featuring colorful, often dissonant harmonies and difficult rhythms. Quite varied in mood.

435 Rodrigo, Joaquin. *Aranjuez, ma Pensée* (French). 1968/c1988 Rodrigo EJR 1784. Text by Victoria Kahmi. Medium B3-G5/B3-D5. *M.* Adapted by the composer from the *Adagio* of his *Concierto de Aranjuez.* Diatonic with mostly stepwise, repetitive melodic motion. Intricate rhythms, yet accessible due to adagio tempo. Very long melodic lines. Extended guitar solo near end of piece.

436 Rodrigo, Joaquin. *Folías Canarias* (Spanish). 1958/c1959 Schott ED 10600. Medium A4-E5/A4-E4. *M.* Song from the Canary Islands. Largely diatonic with stepwise, repetitive melodic motion and uncomplicated rhythms. Spanish melodic traits, such as rapid grace notes, are used. Guitar accompaniment consists mostly of several patterns which are repeated throughout the piece.

437 Rodrigo, Joaquin. *Romance de Durandarte* (Spanish). 1955/c1995 Rodrigo EJR 190174. Medium E4-F5/E4-E5. *M.* Diatonic with mostly stepwise melodic motion and simple, repeated rhythms. Vocal line incorporates elements of Spanish style such as rapid melodic turns. Guitar part consists of a simple melodic motive that is periodically played over an E3 rhythm pattern.

438 Rodrigo, Joaquin. *Tres Canciones Españolas* (Spanish). 1951/c1960 Schott ED 10601. High C♯4-E5/F♯4-D♯5. *M.* Group of three songs (6'). Diatonic with simple rhythms and largely stepwise melodic motion. Strong Spanish folk flavor in terms of text and melody. Strophic in form. Some rapid melodic turns are required. English singing version included. Accessible, repetitive guitar accompaniment.

439 Rodrigo, Joaquin. *Tres Villancicos* (Spanish). 1952/c1959 Schott ED 12376. Text by various authors. Medium D4-F♯5/F♯4-D5. *M.* Group of three

Spanish Christmas folk carols (7'). Varied in mood and tempi. Diatonic with uncomplicated melodic motion and rhythms. Some rapid melodic turns and grace notes. Includes English singing version. Repetitive, active guitar accompaniment.

440 Rodriguez, Rafael Albert. *Cuatro Canciones* (Spanish). c1963 Union UMG19734. Text by Lope de Vega. High C#4-F#5/E4-F5. *M.* Group of four songs (15'). Accessible melodies and rhythms of strong Spanish musical flavor. First song has an extended section of rapid sixteenth-note phrases. Some variation of mood within cycle. Active and fairly challenging guitar accompaniment.

441 Rojas, René. *Canciones Populares* (Spanish). c1984 Venezolanos 19. Text by composer. Medium B3-E5/D3-B4. *E.* Group of three songs (8'). Diatonic and rhythmically simple Spanish folk songs with new, revised accompaniments. Varying moods and tempi. Uncomplicated, repetitive guitar accompaniment.

442 Roland, Claude-Robert. *Ballade de Villon* (French). 1967 Belgium. Text by François Villon. Male C#3-E4/D3-D4. *D.* Atonal, with most vocal phrases consisting of many repeated notes within the range of M3 accompanied by guitar lines which are very dissonant to the voice. Ametrical, with a recitative-like style throughout. Accessible, often sparse guitar part.

443 Rosenfeld, Gerhard. *Abschied* (German). c1971 Neue NM 285. Text by Ralph Knebel. Medium D4-D5/G4-D5. *E.* From the 12-song collection *...und die Liebe braucht ein Dach*, compiled by Helge Jung and Werner Pauli. Simple, diatonic melody in strophic form. Several uncomplicated meter changes. Simple, mostly chordal guitar accompaniment.

444 Rövenstrunck, Bernat. *Katalanisches Liederbuch* (Catalonian). c1976 Trekel T 0602. Text by various authors. High or Medium C4-F5/E4-E5. *D.* Collection of 32 songs of Catalonian origin in terms of text or melody, newly composed or arranged utilizing modern techniques by the composer. Quite varied in terms of musical attributes and difficulty level. A German singing version is also provided for all songs.

445 Ruiter, Wim De. *Four Songs on Poems by e.e. cummings* (English). 1993/c1993 Donemus. Text by e.e. cummings. Soprano F3-D♭6/C4-F#5. *VD.* Group of four songs (15'). Each piece varies greatly in terms of melodic motion, tonality, rhythm, tempo, mood, and accompaniment. Song #1 uses clapping, song #3 is ametrical and has several leaps exceeding two octaves, and song #4 contains complex meter changes.

446 Ruiz-Pipó, Antonio. *Cantos a la Noche* (Spanish). c1971 Berben E. 1519 B. Text by composer. High B♭3-G#5/F#4-E5. *VD.* (8'). Atonal and mostly ametrical. Features brief, detached vocal phrases that are not difficult by themselves, but are independent of and dissonant to the guitar. Requires a wide dynamic range and is quite dramatic at times. Demanding, very expressive guitar.

447 Salzman, Eric. *Verses II.* Mills College Library. High E3-B♭5/F4-G5. *VD.* (12'). Atonal and often ametrical. Voice part consists largely of phonetic sounds on indeterminate pitches. Extensive use of unconventional techniques such as tongue clicking, breathy voice and sustained nonvowel sounds, along with myriad guitar effects.

448 Samuel, Rhian. *Three Songs with Guitar* (English). Andresier 0026. Text by various authors. High A3-A5/F4-G5. *VD.* Group of three songs (12'). Atonal, with largely detached vocal phrases featuring disjunct, chromatic intervals. Utilizes a wide array of dynamics, rhythms, meters, and tempi. Song #3 contains many sustained high notes and an A5-A3 portamento. Varied and substantial guitar part.

449 Sanchez, Blas. *Al Pie de la Cruz del Roque* (Spanish). c1964 Eschig ME 7559. Text by Pedro Ramos. High G#4-F5/A4-E5. *E.* Diatonic with stepwise melodic motion and easy, basic rhythms. Folk-like in its strophic form and simple textual content. The guitar accompaniment is active yet accessible, consisting of mostly eighth-note patterns at a lively tempo. French singing text included.

450 Sanchez, Blas. *Arroro* (Spanish). c1964 Eschig ME 7558. Text by composer. High A3-G5/E4-D5. *M.* Mostly diatonic with accessible melodic motion and rhythms. Essentially a slow piece, it is sectionalized by several tempo variations, along with changes in melody and accompaniment. Active, varied guitar part is largely accompanimental in nature.

451 Sanchez, Blas. *Atardecer en Canarias* (Spanish). 1965/c1966 Choudens A.C. 20.627. Text by composer. Medium D4-G5/F#4-E5. *M.* Tonal with some chromaticism. Mixed, accessible melodic motion and largely repetitive rhythms which contain some subtle yet significant variations. Utilizes a few rapid melodic turns as befitting its Spanish nature. Guitar part challenging at times.

452 Sanchez, Blas. *Ay, Barquita* (Spanish). 1966/c1966 Choudens A.C. 20.268. Text by composer. High D4-A5/D4-F5. *D.* Tonal with some chromaticism. Mostly disjunct melodic motion (intervals of P4 or wider are common) with uncomplicated rhythms in a very fast, lively tempo. Strong Spanish flavor, emphasized by long melismas and forte, sustained "Ay!" on A5 at the end.

453 Sanchez, Blas. *Ingenio* (Spanish). c1964 Eschig ME 7556. Text by composer. High D4-G#5/F#4-E5. *M.* Diatonic with mostly stepwise melodic motion and straightforward rhythms. The piece is divided into several sections, each noted by differing key, meter, tempo, melody and guitar accompaniment. Some grace note ornamentations. Active, quite varied guitar part.

454 Sanchez, Blas. *Nananita Nana* (Spanish). 1966/c1966 Choudens A.C. 20.266. Text by composer. Medium B3-F#5/A4-E5. *M.* A lullaby, with long, simple, legato melodic phrases. Pitches of the vocal line, while consonant with the guitar, are often not doubled in its part. Accompaniment consists solely of repeated thirty-second-note broken chord patterns in an andantino tempo.

455 Sanchez, Blas. *Paisage* (Spanish). 1966/c1966 Choudens A.C. 20.265. Text by composer. Medium D4-F#5/D4-D5. *M.* Mostly diatonic, with straightforward rhythms and melodic motion in an andante con moto setting. The last fourteen measures are quasi-recitative, featuring tremolo guitar chords. Prior to that, the accompaniment consists mostly of Alberti bass patterns.

456 Santórsola, Guido. *Cinco Canciones* (Spanish). 1981/c1982 Berben E. 2406 B. Text by Jesús Silva. High B3-B5/C#4-G5. *D.* Group of five songs (11'45"). Tonal with extensive chromaticism. Many detached vocal phrases of repeated pitches with detailed rhythms, yielding a recitative-like effect. Guitar is most prominent and very demanding, often giving little accompanimental support.

457 Sarmanto, Heikki. *Nellä Laulua* (Finnish). c1982 Fazer FM 06583-9. Text by Aaro Hellaakoski. Low F3-F5/A3-E5. *D.* Cycle of four songs (10'). Diatonic with melodic motion and rhythms that are not excessively complex. The most imposing demand of this work is its wide tessitura, requiring sustained forte tones at extremes of the vocal range. English singing version provided.

458 Satke, Wilfried. *Fragen und Antworten* (German). 1987 composer. Text by Erich Fried. Medium or Low Bb3-C5/D4-C5. *M.* Tonally elusive with unusual, mostly consonant harmonies. Vocal line consists of brief, fragmented phrases that are often disjunct, repetitive, and somewhat chromatic, with many syncopations. Guitar part is largely accompanimental, consisting almost entirely of sixteenth-note broken chords.

459 Satke, Wilfried. *Ein Neues Land Gebe Ich Euch* (German). 1980 composer. Text by Georg Bydlinski. Medium or Low A3-F5/C4-D5. *D.* A Mass in nine movements (30'40"). Mostly uncomplicated, widely varied rhythms and melodic motion in a tonally elusive setting featuring colorful, unusual harmonies with some dissonance. Optional group singing in some passages. Guitar part is often more prominent than the voice.

460 Satke, Wilfried. *13 x von Tieren Singen* (German). 1993 composer. Text by Georg Bydlinski. Medium C4-D5/D4-B4. *E.* Group of 13 short childen's songs (10'). Simple, repetitive melodies that are largely diatonic, accompanied by chordal structures commonly associated with contemporary folk guitar music. Printed chord symbols allow for optional accompaniment by other instruments.

461 Schmidt, Eberhard. *Die Blätter an Meinem Kalender* (German). c1981 Neue NM 415. Text by Peter Hacks from *Der Flohmarkt.* Medium C4-E5/E4-E5. *M.* Cycle of nine short songs interspersed with seven solo guitar interludes (15'). Tonal with chromaticism. Mixed, accessible melodic motion and varied, mostly uncomplicated rhythms. Often light-hearted in mood. Active, substantial guitar part is challenging at times.

462 Schmidt, Lorenz. *Ein Duft von Licht* (German). c1987 Vogt V&F 405a. Text from Japanese haiku. Medium A3-F5/B3-D5. *D.* Cycle of five very short songs (3'). Atonal, consisting of brief, detached vocal phrases with disjunct, chromatic intervals rarely larger than P4. Varied yet uncomplicated rhythms set to generally slow tempi. Intricate guitar part contains much dissonance.

463 Schmidt, Mia. *Die Gestundete Zeit* (German). 1987/c1992 composer. Text by Ingeborg Bachmann. Mezzo G3-G5/A3-D5. *VD.* Atonal, with fragmented, highly disjunct chromatic melodic motion. Intricate rhythms within constantly changing meters and tempi. Wide dynamic range is employed, along with rapid crescendo and decrescendo on sustained notes. Myriad nontraditional techniques are required for both performers.

464 Schmitz, Manfred. *Der Letzte Strahl* (German). c1971 Neue NM 285. Text by Georg Maurer. Tenor F#3-A4/A3-F#4. *M.* From the 12-song collection ...*und die Liebe braucht ein Dach,* compiled by Helge Jung and Werner Pauli. Simple diatonic melody, much of which consists of repeated pitches with eighth-note rhythms. Requires very long (over seven measures) F#4 at end of piece.

465 Schneider, Klaus. *Abendlied* (German). c1971 Neue NM 285. Text by Rainer Kirsch. High D#4-E5/G4-E5. *M.* From the 12-song collection ...*und die Liebe braucht ein Dach,* compiled by Helge Jung and Werner Pauli. Diatonic melody with mostly simple disjunct melodic motion. Some challenging triplet rhythms. Strophic in form. Simple, varied guitar accompaniment.

466 Schneider, Klaus. *Liebeslied* (German). c1971 Neue NM 285. Text by Herribert Schenke. High B3-E5/E4-E5. *E.* From the 12-song collection ...*und die Liebe braucht ein Dach,* compiled by Helge Jung and Werner Pauli. Diatonic melody with uncomplicated disjunct melodic motion. Strophic in form. Simple, repetitious guitar accompaniment.

467 Schneider, Simon. *Im Volkston* (German). 1953/c1953 Helvetia HV 647. Text by various authors. High C4-F5/E4-E5. *E.* Group of six strophic songs (12'). Diatonic with simple, direct melodies. Somewhat varied in mood and tempo. Accessible guitar part is comprised mostly of various conventional chordal accompaniment patterns.

468 Schneider, Simon. *Sechs Lieder* (German). 1953/c1953 Helvetia HV 648. Text by various authors. High B3-F#5/E4-E5. *E.* Group of six strophic songs (12'). Mostly diatonic with simple, unpretentious melodies. Somewhat varied in mood and tempo. Accessible guitar part is comprised mostly of various conventional chordal accompaniment patterns.

469 Sealey, Ray. *A Circle of Tears* (Latin). c1978 Waterloo WCG-313. Text by Betsey Barker Price. High C#4-A5/F#4-G5. *M.* Cycle of seven songs (9'). Mostly diatonic with accessible rhythms and generally stepwise melodic motion. Varied in tempo and mood. Utilizes humming, parlando, glissando, and optional wind chimes. Guitar requires improvisation and unusual sounds such as string squeaks and tapping.

470 Seiber, Matyas. *Four French Folk Songs* (French). c1959 Schott ED 10637. High E4-E5/E4-E5. *M.* Group of four traditional French folk songs with new guitar accompaniments (10'). Varied in mood and tempo; the last song is quite fast and light-hearted. Active, expressive guitar part is somewhat challenging in several brief instances.

471 Sevriens, Jean. *Songs from Diana* (English). 1986/c1990 Donemus. Text by Diana Hedrick. High C#4-Bb5/B4-G5. *D.* Cycle of four songs (12'). Tonal with fairly high tessitura and challenging rhythms due to changing, unusual meters. Mood varies greatly from piece to piece. Spoken passages are intermittently featured. Difficult, active guitar part.

472 Shifrin, Seymour. *A Birthday Greeting* (English). 1976/c1982 APNM. Text by William Shakespeare from *King Lear*, Act 5, Scene 2. Soprano C4-Ab5/Eb4-F#5. *VD.* Atonal with highly disjunct, chromatic melodic motion; intervals generally exceed P4. Utilizes complex rhythms, especially in the guitar. Long, connected vocal phrases. Very demanding guitar part whose rhythms and pitches are usually opposed to the voice.

473 Shore, Clare. *Grave Numbers* (English). 1987/c1987 Schirmer ECS 4604. Text by Blanche Farley. Medium Ab3-Gb5/C#4-D5. *VD.* Cycle of four songs (10'). Atonal with highly disjunct, chromatic melodic motion and varied complex rhythms amidst numerous meter changes. Largely lento settings (except for song #2) of serious, somewhat somber texts. Requires use of chest and breathy voices. Intricate, demanding guitar part.

474 Short, Michael. *Hesperides* (English). Crouch. Text by Robert Herrick. High B3-Gb5/E4-E5. *D.* Cycle of five songs (12'). Tonal with much chromaticism, yielding colorful harmonies that are mostly consonant. Many long, legato vocal lines. Mixed, accessible melodic motion and rhythms in a variety of tempi, meter and moods. Active, substantial guitar part features many diverse sections.

475 Sigurbjörnsson, Thorkell. *Musik* (German). 1992/c1992 Iceland ITM 022-161. Text by Rainer Maria Rilke. Soprano B♭3-G5/F4-F5. *D.* Tonality is based on brief, accessible melodic (and rhythm) sequences in both voice and guitar which are repeated throughout on progressive pitch levels. Uses unusual, constantly changing meters, and features a recitative-like ametrical section.

476 Simoes de Irajá, Inara. *Dentro da Noite* (Spanish). c1957 *Guitar Review* #21. Text by composer. Low G3-E5/A♯3-B4. *M.* Mostly diatonic with mixed, accessible melodic motion. Rhythms are repetitive and generally uncomplicated. The guitar harmonies, along with the melody and rhythms yield a distinctive Spanish folk-like quality. Guitar accompaniment is mostly chordal.

477 Smith, Larry Alan. *An Infant Crying* (English). 1984/c1986 Merion 141-40017. Text by various authors. High D4-A5/E4-F♯5. *D.* Cycle of three songs (22'). Generally accessible vocal phrases sung over guitar lines that are often dissonant, yet imply tonality. Somber, contemplative texts in expressive and varied settings, especially in song #2, which also has a brief narrative passage.

478 Smith Brindle, Reginald. *Two Poems of Manley Hopkins* (English). c1983 Schott ED 11485. Text by Manley Hopkins. Medium B♭3-E5/E4-E5. *VD.* Group of two songs (8'). Atonal with disjunct, fragmented melodic phrases. The first song is ametrical and the second has many meter changes, yet the vocal rhythms in both are not complicated. Difficult guitar part contains many unusual, colorful chords.

479 Solomons, David W. *As Gleams the Rosebud* (English). 1993/c1993 composer. Text by Pierre de Ronsard. Alto or Countertenor B3-B4/B3-A4. *E.* Tonal, with accessible, repetitive melodic motions and rhythms in a plaintive minor setting. Generally long, legato vocal phrases over a primarily chordal guitar accompaniment.

480 Solomons, David W. *Beetles' Wings* (English). 1993/c1993 composer. Text by Audrey Vaughan. Alto or Countertenor E3-E5/B3-B4. *M.* Tonal, with disjunct yet uncomplicated long vocal phrases and accessible rhythms. Harmonically simple construct allows for the predominance of the straightforward love text. Requires a sustained E5 near the end. Guitar consists primarily of whole-note chords and eighth-note arpeggios.

481 Solomons, David W. *A Greek Wassail* (English). 1993/c1993 composer. Text by composer. Alto or Countertenor D4-B4/E4-B♭4. *E.* Simple, lively strophic song in 7/4 with much repetition in terms of melody, rhythms, and guitar accompaniment. The latter consists primarily of diatonic chords either played in block or "oom-pah" configurations.

482 Solomons, David W. *Haiku by Matsuo Basho* (Japanese). 1993/c1993 composer. Text by Matsuo Basho. Low G3-B4/B3-G4. *M.* Tonally elusive and texturally sparse, yielding an ethereal atmosphere often associated with Japanese haiku, which is further reinforced by the ametrical feel brought on by frequently changing meters. In romanized Japanese. The vocal phrases are very repetitive and appear infrequently, while the accessible, lightly textured guitar is featured most prominently.

483 Solomons, David W. *Haviranosan No Haiku* (English). 1996/c1996 composer. Text by Mark Haviland. Alto or Countertenor E3-B♭4/C4-B♭4. *M.* Tonally elusive, yet contains virtually no dissonances. The text and sparse, fragmented texture evoke an ethereal mood associated with haiku, aided by changing meters with much rhythmic freedom. Save for two instances of octave leaps, melody is quite accessible. Accessible, lute-like guitar.

484 Solomons, David W. *Lookin' Just Lookin'* (English). 1995/c1995 composer. Alto or Countertenor A3-D5/C4-C5. *M.* Utilizes many musical idioms most often associated with "pop/folk" music, including syncopations, specific chord progressions, chordal guitar configurations, and topical, light-hearted subject (personal ads).

485 Solomons, David W. *Ludhe Sing* (English). 1993/c1993 composer. Alto or Countertenor F♯3-A4/B3-G4. *M.* A humorous parody based on *Sumer is icumen in,* from the perspective of one who suffers summer allergies. Requires singer to inhale loudly, sigh, and sneeze. Simple, chordal guitar part reinforces the style of the original music.

486 Solomons, David W. *New Troubadour Blues* (English). 1995/c1995 composer. Text by composer. Baritone or Bass E2-E5/B3-B4. *D.* Tonal, with a "pop/blues" approach in its use of melody, harmony, and rhythms. Very wide pitch range, with rapid descents exceeding two octaves; requires secure, sustained E2. Features somewhat intricate syncopations amidst many meter changes. Accessible guitar part is mostly chordal.

487 Solomons, David W. *The Quiet Way You Move Me* (English). 1993/c1993 composer. Text by Neville Frenkiel. Alto or Countertenor C4-C5/C4-G5. *E.* Tonal, with accessible, repetitive melodic motion and rhythms. Simple love text set to brief vocal phrases over an almost constant sixteenth-note arpeggio guitar accompaniment. Humming required at the end.

488 Solomons, David W. *Sentimental Song* (English). 1993/c1993 composer. Text by Vahan Teryan. Alto or Countertenor A♭3-D5/A3-D5. *M.* Largely diatonic with smooth, accessible vocal lines set to a gently flowing tempo. Uncomplicated syncopated rhythms in both parts and broken-chord guitar patterns mimic contemporary folk music. Straightforward, repetitive guitar part is essentially accompanimental in nature.

489 Solomons, David W. *Wrong Side of the Door* (English). 1994/c1994 composer. Text by P. Maertens. Low G#3-B♭4/A3-A4. *M.* Tonal, light-hearted song about a demanding cat, from its perspective. Accessible melodic motion and rhythms, despite many meter changes. Glissandi and purring sounds are required.

490 Sønstevold, Gunnar. *5 Sånger til Tekst av Tarjei Vesaas* (Norwegian). 1964 Norway S 400 SØN. Text by Tarjei Vesaas. High A3-B♭5/C4-G5. *VD.* Group of five songs (18'). Atonal with many chromatic, very disjunct vocal lines. Meters change frequently, yet rhythms are largely undemanding. Much variety in tempo within and between each song. Sparse guitar uses mostly single-note lines and dissonant two- and three-voiced chords.

491 Sörenson, Torsten. *Tre Medititiva Sånger* (Swedish). 1980 Sweden T-2873. Text by Helge Jedenberg. Soprano D4-G5/D4-F5. *D.* Group of three songs (10'). Atonal with mixed chromatic melodic motion, often in long, connected phrases that are dissonant to the guitar. Varied yet not complex rhythms in overall slow tempi. Active guitar part in first two songs; the third consists almost solely of half-note chords.

492 Souris, André. *Louison, Embarquons-nous.* Belgium. Baritone G2-E4/D3-D4. *M.* The song is wordless and in strophic form. Diatonic with mostly stepwise melodic motion. Numerous changes of compound meters, yet rhythms are not difficult. The very simple guitar part consists almost exclusively of single notes on a repeated rhythm pattern.

493 Spedding, Frank. *Four Scots Songs* (English). 1970 Scotland. Tenor D3-A4/E3-E4. *M.* Group of four songs (10'). Traditional Scottish folk melodies in new settings. Varied in mood and tempo. Song #3 employs many meters, including 7/8 and 5/4, and briefly features separate meters for each player. Accessible, interesting guitar accompaniments.

494 Spedding, Frank. *The Man with the Axe* (French). 1971 Scotland. Text by Alfred Jarry. Tenor C3-A4/E3-F#4. *VD.* Cycle of four songs (12'). Atonal with short, detached vocal phrases of complex, disjunct melodic motion. Many intricate rhythms and meter changes. Utilizes a wide range of dynamics, often shifting abruptly. Contains brief passages of sprechstimme and falsetto.

495 Stefánsson, Finnur Torfi. *Morgunn* (Icelandic). 1990/c1990 Iceland ITM 057-023. Text by Ari Jósepsson. Countertenor G3-A5/C4-E5. *VD.* Atonal with complex, sometimes highly disjunct melodic motion. Meters change often, and many of the rhythms are intricate, most notably in the guitar. Generally slow, the piece features several subtle changes in tempo. Dissonant, independent guitar part.

496 Strindberg, Henrik. *Det Första Kvädet om Gudrun* (Swedish). 1987/c1988 Reimers ER 101144. Text by Björn Collinder from *Den Poetiska Eddan.* Mezzo A3-A5/A3-C5. *D.* (19'). Mostly diatonic based on a key signature containing only F# and G#. Opens with a 4-minute recitation, and then features long, lyric, generally accessible vocal phrases. The guitar part, which calls for unusual tuning, is rather active and much more complex than the voice.

497 Strobl, Bruno. *In dem Land, dem Verhüllten* (German). 1987 Studio. Text by various authors. Mezzo E3-G♭5/G3-D5. *VD.* Cycle of six songs (12'). Atonal, with often fragmented, highly disjunct chromatic melodic motion. Intricate rhythms in changing meters; ametricality often used. Nontraditional techniques include glissando, sprechgesang, and speaking. Very challenging guitar employs diverse playing effects.

498 Strutt, Dal. *Interludes I & II* (English). c1991 Roeginga. Text by composer from *Marshland.* Medium A♭3-F5/D4-E♭5. *VD.* Group of two songs (10'). Atonal with mixed, chromatic melodic motion, commonly dissonant with the guitar. Rhythms in both parts are often independent of each other. Song #2 contains unusual 9/8 groupings. Many octave doublings in guitar yield sparse texture.

499 Stucky, Rodney. *Five Spirituals* (English). c1995 Southern V-98. Mezzo A3-G#5/E4-E5. *M.* Group of five songs (11'). Traditional American spiritual melodies arranged with new accompaniments that utilize some colorful harmonies in a firmly tonal setting. The generally accessible guitar part features varied settings, each helping to set the appropriate mood within the song.

500 Sundstrøm, Andy. *God Morgen Æblerose* (Danish). 1981/c1982 composer, also Tingluti. Text by Ellen Heiberg. Various ranges F#3-A5/A3-B4. *E.* Collection of 19 songs, all of which have been written with simple, contemporary folk-like strophic melodies and guitar accompaniment patterns. Each song varies in pitch range and generally encompasses no more than an octave.

501 Sundstrøm, Andy. *Her Vil Ties, Her Vil Bies* (Danish). 1994 composer. Text by Hans Adolf Brorson. Medium C4-C5/C4-B4. *E.* Diatonic with mostly stepwise melodic motion and simple rhythms in strophic form.

Very accessible guitar accompaniment, featuring mostly block and broken chord patterns of basic, traditional progressions.

502 Sundstrøm, Andy. *Kom Regn af Det Høje* (Danish). 1994 composer. Text by Hans Adolf Brorson. Medium A3-C5/D4-B4. *E.* Mostly diatonic with accessible melodic motion and simple rhythms in strophic form. Guitar accompaniment is uncomplicated and consists primarily of block and broken chord patterns of common traditional progressions.

503 Sundstrøm, Andy. *Sange til "Hans Kohlhas"* (Danish). 1978 composer. Text by Christian Koch from *Hans Kohlhas.* Low G3-C5/A3-A4. *D.* Group of 10 songs (20'). Tonal, with largely diatonic, stepwise melodic motion accompanied by a more chromatic guitar part that contains occasional dissonances. Meter changes are common, yet rhythms are not complex. Straightforward, often chordal guitar.

504 Surinach, Carlos. *Prayers* (English). 1973/c1973 AMP 7302-7. Text by Michel Quoist. Medium B3-G5/E4-D5. *D.* Cycle of three songs (7'), featuring light-hearted texts dealing with aspects of modern American society. Tonal with some chromaticism (mostly in guitar). Uncomplicated melodic motion is merged with speech-like rhythms in various tempi. Substantial, active guitar.

505 Suter, Robert. *My True Love Hath My Heart, and I Have His* (English). 1983/c1996 Müller. Text by various pre-20th-century English authors. Soprano G#3-C6/D4-Ab5. *VD.* Cycle of five songs (16'). Atonal, with much highly disjunct, chromatic melodic motion in a mix of short and long vocal phrases. Diverse meter and rhythm patterns; last song is ametrical. Varied and challenging guitar is often fragmented, and has several solo preludes and postludes.

506 Sveinsson, Atli Heimir. *Prayer* (English). 1989/c1989 Iceland ITM 002-096. Text by Sören Kierkegaard. Countertenor G#3-Eb5/B3-C#5. *D.* Tonally elusive in a largely nonchromatic setting featuring long, lyric melodies with mixed, mostly accessible motion. Ametrical, with an ad libitum irregularity to the beat. Many unusual grace notes. Single-note guitar part is similar in style to the voice.

507 Symonds, Norman. *Lament* (English). 1962/c1972 Canada MV 1102 S988la. Text by John Reeves. Low G#3-C#5/G#3-B4. *M.* Tonal, featuring a slow, legato, yet rhythmically exacting vocal line that is often repetitive. Contains long vocalise in middle section. Somber mood, as implied by the work's title, aided by simple sequential guitar patterns that are repeated alternately throughout the piece.

508 Tarragó, Graciano. *Canciones Populares Españolas, Vol. 1* (Spanish). c1962 Union UMG19637. Text by various authors. High B3-G5/G4-E5. *M.*

Collection of 15 traditional Spanish folk songs with revised, modern guitar accompaniments. Voice part occasionally requires melismas and strong, dramatic high notes. Contains a wide variety of moods and tempi. Active yet accessible guitar parts.

509 Tarragó, Graciano. *Cuatro Canciones Populares Catalana* (Spanish). c1963 Union UMG20181. High C#4-E5/E4-E5. *M.* Group of four traditional folk songs (10') from the Catalan region of Spain, with new accompaniments. Varying tempi and moods within and between pieces. Active guitar part is not complicated.

510 Tate, Brian. *Three Pastorales* (English). 1978/c1979 Berandol BER 1786. Text by various authors. Soprano B3-A5/E4-E5. *M.* Group of three songs (10'). Largely diatonic with uncomplicated melodic motion in a lyrical setting. Several meter changes are featured, yet rhythms are not difficult. Each song differs in mood and tempo. Guitar part is generally accessible throughout.

511 Tate, Phyllis. *Trois Chanson Tristes* (French). c1974 Oxford. Text by various authors. High E4-B♭5/E4-E5. *D.* Group of three. Old French songs (8') set to new accompaniments that are frequently dissonant yet tonal. The guitar part is quite varied and challenging, and often more prominent than the voice due to the simple, strophic nature of the melodies.

512 Tate, Phyllis. *Two Ballads* (English). c1974 Oxford. Text by various authors. Mezzo G3-F#5/C4-E♭5. *D.* Group of two songs (8'). Vocal part generally consists of tonally chromatic, repeated phrases of narrow tessitura set to simple rhythms. However, very wide intervals are abruptly inserted at times. Texts are of a simple folk quality. Accessible guitar interacts well with voice.

513 Taylor, Ian. *¡Ay! Despertad* (Spanish). c1987 English 2010 Q. Text by Fray Luis de Leon. Soprano B3-B5/E4-F5. *VD.* (8'). Atonal with much disjunct, chromatic melodic motion. Quite varied in tempi and dynamics, yielding expressive, often dramatic sections. Requires a sustained, fortissimo B♭5 and B5, and sprechstimme is used frequently. Intricate, difficult guitar part has several ametrical solo passages.

514 Thiriet, Maurice. *Démons et Merveilles* (French). c1959 Choudens A.C. 19.943. Text by Jacques Prévert. Medium C4-D5/D4-C5. *E.* From the score of the movie *Les Visiteurs du Soir.* Diatonic with simple melodic motion and rhythms in an andante 6/8 meter, producing long, flowing legato phrases. Very accessible guitar part consists almost exclusively of sustained, arpeggiated traditional chords.

515 Thomas, Juan Maria. *Canciones Populares Mallorquinas* (Spanish). c1962 Union UMG19733. High C#4-A5/E4-E5. *M.* Group of four songs

(10'). Distinctive traditional Spanish folk song qualities in terms of melody, harmony and text. Many grace notes in second song, otherwise the vocal lines are musically quite accessible. Guitar arrangement is simple and somewhat sparse.

516 Thomson, Virgil. *What Is It?* (English). 1980/c1981 Presser 111-40091. Text by Thomas Campion. High E4-E5/G4-D5. *M.* Mostly diatonic with accessible, mixed melodic motion and rhythms in an andante 6/8 setting. Guitar part, based on conventional harmonies, is equally prominent due to its active, nonstop accompaniment which can be challenging at times.

517 Thorkelsdóttir, Mist. *Dance* (Icelandic). 1985/c1992 Iceland ITM 048-002. Text by Steinn Steinarr. Medium A♭3-A♯5/D4-D5. *D.* (8'). Atonal, with many repeated vocal patterns featuring highly disjunct melodic motion. Meter changes make common rhythmic figures challenging. The guitar is more prominent and difficult, and is given several substantial, contrasting solo sections.

518 Tippett, Michael. *Songs for Achilles* (English). 1961/c1964 Schott ED 10874. Tenor C♯3-B♭4/G3-G4. *D.* Cycle of three songs (12'). Atonal, and very diverse in terms of musical qualities. Song #1 features long dramatic vocal lines over a rapid guitar part. Song #3 has lengthy guitar solos at the beginning and end, and a recitative-like middle vocal section.

519 Utting, Craig. *Two Old French Songs* (several languages). 1984/c1984 composer. Medium B3-E5/F♯4-D5. *D.* Group of two songs (3') in French. Second verse of song #1 is English translation of first verse. First song features accessible, sometimes chromatic melody over guitar chords that often superimpose major and minor. Song #2 is atonal, with disjunct melody over long, repeated dissonant chords.

520 Valle, Adela Del. *Campera* (Spanish). * Romero 7017. Medium D4-E5/F4-D5. *E.* Diatonic and in strophic form. Features simple, mostly quarter note rhythms in both parts and mixed melodic motion that rarely exceeds M3. Guitar accompaniment has an eight-measure introduction in eighth notes, then plays mostly quarter-note (or longer) chords.

521 Valle, Adela Del. *El Ciprés* (Spanish). * Romero 7021. Medium E4-E5/G4-D5. *E.* In strophic form and mostly diatonic, with largely stepwise melodic motion. The introduction contains a simple eight-measure guitar solo, followed by verses of varied uncomplicated melodic phrases repeated over a continuous dotted rhythm accompaniment.

522 Valle, Adela Del. *Nenía* (Spanish). * Romero 7032. High D4-F5/A4-E5. *E.* Diatonic and in strophic form. Features simple half- and quarter-note rhythms in both parts and mostly stepwise melodic motion. Guitar part has a nine-measure introduction that states the melody, then plays a simple quarter-note chordal accompaniment.

523 Van, Jeffrey. *Come Away, Death* (English). 1966/c1978 Cavata CMP 1004. Text by William Shakespeare. High F4-A5/G4-E5. *M.* Diatonic with long, lyric vocal lines of mixed, accessible melodic motion and simple rhythms, despite meter changes. Some phrases occur where the pitch stays between F5 and A5. Guitar is mostly chordal, containing some colorful seventh chords and ninth chords.

524 Vandermaesbrugge, Max. *Cinq "Chansons de Pancruche"* (French). 1964/c1975 Belgium 75-118. Text by Paul Weyemberg. Baritone B2-G4/E3-E4. *VD.* Tonal with much chromaticism. Contains many long, lyric vocal lines of mixed, mostly accessible melodic motion. Rhythms can be rather challenging due to subtly changing patterns and virtually constant meter changes, often via abstract meters such as 2½/4.

525 Vertlieb, Phil. *Six Haiku* (English). c1975 General GE 41. Text by various authors. Soprano B3-A5/E4-E5. *D.* Group of six songs (8'). Diatonic with lyrical vocal phrases of mixed melodic motion. Several songs change meter frequently, yet rhythms are not complicated. Mood varies greatly from piece to piece. Challenging and rather prominent guitar part.

526 Viitala, Mauri. *An Lina* (German). 1986/c1992 Finland 12802. Text by Johann Wolfgang Goethe. Medium A3-E5/D4-D5. *E.* Sequential, long vocal lines with accessible diatonic melodic motion and harmonies. Elementary rhythms in a *grazioso* 9/8 setting in ABA form. Active, varied guitar part presents interesting countermelodies to the voice.

527 Viitala, Mauri. *Die Spröde* (German). 1986/c1992 Finland 12801. Text by Johann Wolfgang Goethe. High E4-G5/G4-E5. *E.* ABA form, using long vocal lines with disjunct yet sequential melodic motion and elementary rhythms in a lively *con moto* tempo. Climaxes to G5 on last note. Simple, yet varied guitar part which primarily displays the traditional harmonic framework of the song.

528 Villa-Lobos, Heitor. *Aria* (Portuguese). c1954 AMP DST9004. Text by Ruth V. Corréa. Soprano E4-Bb5/A4-G5. *D.* Begins with a lengthy and difficult florid vocalise, then goes into a quasi-recitative section, and concludes with a similar but shorter version of the first section. English translation for singing provided. Repetitive accompaniment patterns in guitar.

529 Vishnick, Martin. *Salop Galop* (English). 1986/c1986 composer. Text by Philip Burchett. High C4-G5/E4-D5. *E.* Simple 6/8 rhythms in a lively allegro tempo. Mostly diatonic, with a few uncomplicated yet unexpected chromatic tones. Consists of three verses, the last of which varies melodically at its end. Guitar accompaniment is active and varied, yet accessible.

530 Vishnick, Martin. *El Silencio* (Spanish). c1994 composer. Text by Federico García Lorca. Mezzo G3-A5/D4-D5. *M.* Tonal, in ABA-Coda form with mixed melodic motion that is accessible despite wide pitch range. Uncomplicated rhythms in a largely slow, sedate setting. Guitar part is quite varied yet not difficult, and helps to contribute to the overall mood.

531 Vishnick, Martin. *Soundwave* (English). 1986/c1986 composer. Text by Isobel Thrilling. Medium B3-G#5/E4-D5. *M.* Mostly diatonic, yet vocal line can be challenging due to key changes and largely disjunct melodic motion with several wide intervals (equal to or exceeding m7). Alternates between 3/4 and 6/8 in a lento tempo. Guitar part is accessibly active and primarily accompanimental.

532 Vishnick, Martin. *This Aye Neet* (English). 1994/c1994 composer. Text by Tony Harrisin. High D4-F#5/E4-E5. *E.* Diatonic with uncomplicated sequential melodic phrases in a lyric allegretto setting. Simple chordal guitar accompaniment complements the vocal line both rhythmically and melodically.

533 Vocht, Lodewijk de. *Tijl-Liederen* (Dutch). c1968 composer. Text by Bert Peleman. Baritone B2-F#4/E3-E4. *M.* Group of nine songs (25'), the first being a rapid, challenging guitar solo. The vocal pieces are essentially diatonic, featuring uncomplicated, repetitive melodies in strophic form with mostly chordal accompaniment. Tempi are generally slow throughout.

534 Walker, Gwyneth. *After All White Horses Are in Bed* (English). c1979 composer. Text by e.e. cummings. High D♭4-A5/E♭4-E5. *M.* Tonal with some chromaticism. Uncomplicated, lyric vocal lines of mixed melodic motion and simple rhythms, with much repetition. Requires a soft A5 at very end. Maintains a constantly tranquil mood, aided by the guitar's often arpeggiated accompaniment.

535 Walker, Gwyneth. *As a Branch in May* (English). 1988/c1993 Schirmer ECS 4309. Text by composer. Medium D4-G5/D4-B4. *E.* Diatonic with a simple, contemporary folk-like melody and text, and is most appropriate for a wedding ceremony. Features a brief, unmetered a cappella section at the end. Varied yet accessible guitar accompaniment.

536 Walker, Gwyneth. *The Nocturnal Nibbler* (English). c1979 composer. Text by composer. Medium A3-F#5/D4-E5. *M.* Tonal with chromaticism, featuring accessible rhythms and mostly stepwise melodic motion. Humorous text set to a lively, fast tempo using different uncomplicated meters. Active guitar part reinforces light-heartedness through varied timbres and settings.

537 Walker, Gwyneth. *Still* (English). c1979 composer. Text by composer. Medium C4-E5/E4-E5. *M.* Diatonic, somewhat fragmented vocal phrases of simple melodic motion and rhythm, many of which are repeated throughout the song. Romantic text set to a gentle, moderato tempo. Guitar part is primarily accompanimental, with many repeated arpeggio patterns.

538 Walker, Gwyneth. *Three Songs for Baritone and Guitar* (English). 1986 composer. Text by various authors. Baritone A2-G4/D3-D4. *M.* Group of three contrasting songs (10'). Song #1 is a jaunty setting of Elizabethan text with challenging meter changes. Songs #2 and #3 are more tranquil; the former features a pastoral text by A. E. Housman, while the latter is a wedding song with words by the composer.

539 Walker, Gwyneth. *When You Are Old* (English). c1983 composer. Text by George Mackay Brown. Baritone B♭2-E4/F♯3-D4. *D.* Tonal with chromaticism. Many long vocal lines of mostly disjunct motion, often mildly dissonant to the guitar. Vocal rhythms are irregular, yielding a speech-like effect. Guitar lends a sedate mood by repeating a simple rhythm with varied, unusual harmonies.

540 Walton, William. *Anon. In Love* (English). c1960 Oxford OUP 157. Text from *The English Galaxy of Shorter Poems*. Tenor C3-B♭4/E3-F♯4. *D.* Cycle of six songs (9'30"), set to 16th- and 17th-century love poems. Tonal with accessible rhythms. Varied in terms of chromaticism and melodic motion; song #1 is notably chromatic and disjunct. Sprightly and sometimes risqué. Diverse, stimulating guitar part.

541 Weiss, Ferdinand. *4 Frühlings- und Liebeslieder aus den "Carmina Burana"* (German). 1978 composer. High or Medium D4-G5/A4-F5. *D.* Group of four songs (9'). Often tonally ambiguous, with many long, legato, chromatic melodies of mixed motion and conventional rhythms. Diverse tempi and moods. Prominent and active guitar part often features unusual yet consonant harmonies, and is crucial in setting ambience of each song.

542 Wheeler, Scott. *Serenata* (English). 1991/c1991 Wheeler. Text by Mark Van Doren from selected poems of *Morning Worship*. Tenor E3-B4/G3-G4. *D.* Cycle of five songs (10'). Tonal with some chromaticism, yielding vocal lines of varied, accessible melodic motion that are generally lyric. Diverse moods and tempi. The last two songs require sustained high notes (G♯4-B4) at various dynamic levels. Some challenging, playful rhythms. Accessible guitar part is often thinly textured, thus lending a feeling of lightness throughout.

543 Wichman, Roald. *Songs, Ballads and Lieder* (several languages). c1979 Gyldendal. Text by various authors. Medium F♯3-F♯5/D4-B4. *E.* Collection of 29 songs either in English or German, featuring very simple diatonic melodies. The guitar part, while varying from song to song, is always uncomplicated and strictly accompanimental.

544 Williamson, Malcolm. *Three Shakespeare Songs* (English). c1973 Weinberger. Text by William Shakespeare from various plays. High C4-A♭5/E4-F5. *D.* Group of three songs (10'). #1 uses traditional harmonies in an allegretto setting with accessible vocal phrases and repeated guitar patterns. Song #2 is a cappella and tonally elusive, with chromatic, disjunct phrases. Song #3 features largo chords shifting from major to minor while vocal line does likewise, but at opposing times. Can be for piano; written on 2 staves.

545 Wills, Arthur. *A Woman in Love* (English). c1987 Brunton. Text by Kathleen Raine. Alto G3-G5/G3-G5. *D.* Cycle of three songs (8'). Tonal with chromaticism, featuring many wide vocal leaps, often in excess of an octave. However, contrasting motion often yields well-balanced melodic contours. Varying moods and tempi. Active, somewhat challenging guitar part.

546 Winters, Geoffrey. *Three Herrick Songs* (English). 1970/c1975 Anglian ANMS 32. Text by Robert Herrick. Medium D4-E5/E4-D5. *D.* Group of three songs (6'). Atonal with long, lyric phrases of mixed melodic motion. Dissonances are not harsh, and the guitar often supports the vocal pitch. Uncomplicated rhythms in spite of meter changes. Overall moderato tempi. Varied, expressive guitar part.

547 Wishart, Peter. *A Barber* (English). 1965/c1965 New York Public Library. Text by Sir John Suckling. High D4-G5/F♯4-E5. *M.* Tonal with some chromaticism. Melodic motion is often stepwise, yet there are some disjunct passages with very wide intervals. Easy rhythms, despite alternating 2/4 and 3/8 meters. Humorous text. Guitar plays many simple, repetitive single-note passages.

548 Wishart, Peter. *A Sleepe Song* (English). 1957/c1965 New York Public Library. Text by Sidney Dobell. High E4-A5/E4-E5. *D.* Atonal with many highly disjunct phrases that are often dissonant with the guitar. Long, syncopated vocal lines in an andante tempo yield an ametrical effect, helping to enhance the text's lullaby theme. Guitar part is developed from its opening three-note motive.

549 Wistuba-Alvarez, Vladimir. *Bolera Antica (1981).* 1992/c1992 Finland 12709. Soprano F4-C♯6/G4-A5. *D.* No text or vocal instructions are provided. Tonal, with mostly diatonic melodies and accompaniment, the latter doubling the vocal line throughout. High tessitura, with several passages consistently staying at or above G5. Uncomplicated, repetitive rhythms, despite many unnotated meter changes. Accessible, straightforward guitar.

550 Wistuba-Alvarez, Vladimir. *En Ti la Tierra* (Spanish). 1988/c1988 Finland 10594. Text by Pablo Neruda from *Versos del Capitán.* High E4-A5/G4-G5. *M.* Diatonic with long vocal phrases of mostly smooth melodic motion (contains one rapid M9 leap of G4-A5). Largely fast rhythms and frequent meter changes which are not difficult. Often high tessitura. Guitar consists primarily of broken and block chords, and features a brief pizzicato introduction.

551 Wistuba-Alvarez, Vladimir. *Escribana V: para Recordar a Simón Rodriguez* (Spanish). 1994/c1994 Finland 13401. Text by Pablo Neruda from *La Tarde sobre los Tejados* from *Crepesculario*. Soprano D♭4-A5/G4-G5. *VD.* Atonal, yet piece concludes with a strongly tonal ending. Features slow, long, disjunct chromatic vocal lines that are often dissonant to the guitar. Unspecified meters that change frequently yield difficult rhythms. Challenging, very active guitar has a substantial ad libitum solo introduction.

552 Wistuba-Alvarez, Vladimir. *Las Manzanas que Crecen Oyendo el Agua Pura...* (Spanish). 1981/c1981 Finland 12125. Text by Pablo Neruda from *Soneto V de Cien Sonetos de Amor*. High E4-A5/B♭4-G5. *D.* Tonally elusive through the use of mostly unusual diatonic chords and progressions. Melodic motion is accessible, aided by limited but high tessitura. Constant meter changes, not notated (along with tempo), yield challenging rhythms. Guitar part is repetitive and primarily accompanimental.

553 Wistuba-Alvarez, Vladimir. *Yo Soy...el Errante Poeta...* (Spanish). Finland 10593. Text by Pablo Neruda. High G4-B5/B4-G5. *M.* Mostly diatonic with long, sustained vocal phrases of smooth melodic motion and accessible rhythms in 6/8. Relatively high tessitura. Simple, flowing guitar accompaniment.

554 Wordsworth, William. *Psalm* (English). 1984 Scotland. Text from various Christian psalms. High D4-A5/B4-G#5. *VD.* Atonal with mixed melodic motion and varied, rapid rhythms in a lively con moto tempo. Features an ametrical introduction of phonetic sounds and fragmented guitar phrases. Requires many forte, exuberant high notes. Challenging guitar is fast and very active.

555 Wuorinen, Charles. *Psalm 39* (English). 1979/c1979 Peters P66819. Baritone F2-F4/A2-D4. *VD.* (11'). Atonal with highly disjunct, complex melodic motion and many difficult rhythms and meters. Vocal phrases often consist of long, connected passages, some of which are melismatic and very intricate. Challenging, varied guitar is equally as prominent.

556 Yarmolinsky, Ben. *Anecdote of the Jar* (English). c1995 Ben Yar. Text by Wallace Stevens. High or Medium B3-D5/D4-B5. *E.* Tonal, with a folk sensibility due to its plain, pastoral text about Tennessee and its simple, repetitious melody largely based on a pentatonic scale. Simple, straightforward guitar accompaniment.

557 Yarmolinsky, Ben. *Bernstein Songs* (English). c1994 Ben Yar. Text by Charles Bernstein. High or Medium B3-E5/D4-D5. *M.* Group of six songs

(18'). Tonal, with frequent references to folk style in terms of guitar accompaniment patterns and vocal melodies. Sometimes abstract lyrics. Generally animated tempi throughout, and varied in mood. Guitar parts are usually repetitive and subservient to the voice.

558 Yarmolinsky, Ben. *Coda from Briggflats* (English). c1993 Ben Yar. Text by Basil Bunting. High or Medium C4-E5/E4-D4. *M.* Modal tonality and alternations between 3/4 and 6/8 yield a notable Spanish flavor. Uncomplicated, often sequential vocal phrases in a lively tempo. Repetitive guitar part is mostly chordal in design and accompanimental in nature.

559 Yarmolinsky, Ben. *Come In* (English). c1996 Ben Yar. Text by Robert Frost. High or Medium C4-E5/D4-D5. *D.* Mostly diatonic, with brief vocal phrases of relatively smooth melodic motion. Challenging rhythms due to changing unusual meters, such as 7/16, 14/16, and 15/16. Active guitar accompaniment.

560 Yarmolinsky, Ben. *Deutsch Songs* (English). c1993 Ben Yar. Text by Babette Deutsch. Medium B3-E5/B3-C5. *M.* Group of two songs (5'). Mostly diatonic, with accessible, repetitive vocal phrases. Both songs are rather animated. Song #1 features alternating measures of 6/8 and 2/4 with a lively, constant accompaniment. Song #2 is strophic, and is somewhat more melodically disjunct than the first song. Uncomplicated guitar is primarily accompanimental.

561 Yarmolinsky, Ben. *DiPalma Songs* (English). c1995 Ben Yar. Text by Ray DiPalma. High or Medium A3-E5/E4-D5. *D.* Group of six songs (14'). The only song notably longer than 1½ minutes is *penny paper* (3'+). Tonal with accessible melodic motion. Varied rhythms and meters produce some challenging sections. Largely obtuse text helps to yield diverse moods and tempi. Active, subservient guitar.

562 Yarmolinsky, Ben. *Gorey Songs* (English). c1993 Ben Yar. Text by Edward Gorey. High or Medium C#4-G5/E4-D5. *M.* Group of two songs (6'). Light-hearted texts about the supernatural. Song #1 has mostly stepwise vocal phrases, and a light Spanish feel from its modality and alternating 6/8, 3/4, and 4/4 meters. Song #2 is much more chromatic and disjunct, yet the melodies are often sequential and strongly supported by the guitar. Song #1 features a sustained fortissimo G5 at the end.

563 Yarmolinsky, Ben. *Lear Songs* (English). c1992 Ben Yar. Text by Edward Lear. High or Medium A3-E5/B3-C5. *M.* Group of two strophic songs (5'). Tonal, with accessible, unaffected vocal phrases of moderate chromaticism in light-hearted tempi. The first song is set to Lear's well-known *The Owl and the Pussycat*, the second to *The Jumblies*. Uncomplicated, accompanimental guitar part.

564 Yarmolinsky, Ben. *Next to Nothing* (English). c1993 Ben Yar. Text by Paul Bowles. High or Medium B3-E5/D4-D5. *M.* Tonal with chromaticism, yielding accessible, often brief vocal phrases of varied melodic motion and rhythms. Text is a cynically humorous depiction of one's self-perception of worthlessness. Simple, repetitious guitar provides harmonic framework.

565 Yarmolinsky, Ben. *No Longer Very Clear* (English). c1994 Ben Yar. Text by John Ashbery. High or Medium C4-F5/E4-E♭5. *D.* Tonal with some chromaticism. Short vocal phrases of varied melodies and rhythms set in changing, sometimes complex meters yield a spontaneous speech-like feel. Requires use of "quasi-falsetto." The text and the ambience is masculine; several phrases could be altered to accommodate a female singer, but it seems best-suited overall for a male voice.

566 Yarmolinsky, Ben. *One in a Million* (English). 1996/c1996 Ben Yar. Text by composer. High or Medium B3-G5/D4-D5. *E.* Simple, harmonically traditional piece written by the composer to describe his feelings toward his inamorata. Utilizes much sequential repetition in the melody. Features sustained G5 at the conclusion. An altering of the text in mm. 11-12 could allow the work to be sung by anyone.

567 Yarmolinsky, Ben. *Salute* (English). 1995/c1995 Ben Yar. Text by James Schuyler. High or Medium C#4-E5/E4-C#5. *E.* Short, light-hearted tonal piece with animated accompaniment. Accessible syncopations in both voice and guitar, the latter almost continuously due to to its highly repetitive patterns.

568 Yarmolinsky, Ben. *Shakespeare Songs* (English). c1992 Ben Yar. Text by William Shakespeare from *Much Ado About Nothing*. High or Medium D4-E♭5/E4-D5. *M.* Group of two songs (6') with optional but recommended flute (or other) obbligato. Song #2 essentially strophic. Mostly diatonic with animated vocal lines, yielding a simple gaiety often found in Elizabethan music. Accessible rhythms amidst meter changes. Active, accompanimental guitar part.

569 Yarmolinsky, Ben. *She Set Him Free* (English). c1993 Ben Yar. Text by William Pillin. Medium B3-C4/D4-B♭4. *M.* Tonal, with accessible and often repetitive melodic motion and rhythms in a flowing, breezy tempo. Many meter changes at beginning and end of piece. Topical text is of a somewhat sardonic sexual nature. Uncomplicated guitar part consists of several repeated accompanimental patterns.

570 Yarmolinsky, Ben. *She Went Away (On Valentine's Day)* (English). c1994 Ben Yar. Text by Dan Valentine. High or Medium C4-E5/D4-B♭4. *M.* Brief, humorous song in a bluesy style about a jilted lover (as explained in the song's title). Chromaticism appropriate to the style is employed. By substituting the word "he" for "she" in the title and throughout the song, the piece would be appropriate for a female singer.

571 Yarmolinsky, Ben. *She'll Be Comin' Round* (English). c1993 Ben Yar. Text by James Sherry. Medium C#4-Eb5/E4-D5. *M.* Tonal, with accessible, repetitive melodic motion and rhythms. Many of the phrases begin with the music and words to *She'll Be Comin' Round the Mountain,* but then notably deviate, especially in the text, which often becomes abstract. Almost constant "oom-pah" guitar accompaniment.

572 Yoghurtjian, James. *Colorado Trail* (English). c1959 *Guitar Review* #23. Medium B3-D5/D4-A4. *E.* Brief song (22 measures) with a simple, diatonic folk-like melody and text. Leisurely slow tempo, yet forward motion is maintained by the guitar's virtually constant sixteenth-note accompaniment, which is relatively more challenging than the vocal melody.

573 Young, David. *Ninazu.* 1993/c1994 Red House. High or Medium G3-A#5/C4-F#5. *VD.* From the collection *Guitar Plus One.* Atonal, with mostly long melodic lines of smooth chromaticism set to seemingly phonetic sounds (instructions not provided). Slow tempo with constant meter and dynamic changes, and very uncommon rhythmic subdivisions. Features quarter tones and other nontraditional techniques, especially in the very demanding guitar part.

574 Yun, Isang. *Gagok* (Korean). 1972/c1976 Bote bb 1245. High or Medium E4-F5/E4-F5. *VD.* Notated vocal line to this atonal piece is restricted to the notes on lines of the treble clef (EGBDF), presented in numerous rhythm and dynamic combinations. Korean sounds are presented via German transliteration. Many nontraditional techniques are employed in both parts, and are especially prominent in the guitar, which is highly varied in that regard.

575 Yupanqui, Atahualpa. *Colleccion de Atahualpa Yupanqui* (Spanish). c1974 Gendai. Text by Aaro Hellaakoski. Low G#3-E5/B3-B4. *E.* Collection of guitar music by the composer which includes six strophic songs of simple diatonicism. Japanese is intermixed with Spanish on some songs. Easy guitar part generally consists of common accompaniment patterns that are repeated throughout.

576 Zbinden, Julien François. *Blasons des Fleurs* (French). 1959/c196? Foetisch MPF 562. High E4-A5/A4-E5. *M.* Cycle of six songs (13'). Tonal with chromaticism, employing accessible melodies and rhythms of a distinctive, contemporary French nature in contrasting moods and tempi. Guitar part is varied but not difficult.

Bibliography

Apel, W., ed. (1969). *Harvard Dictionary of Music*. 2d ed. Cambridge MA: Belknap Press of Harvard University Press.

Appleby, W. M. (1951). "Song and Guitar in Britain." *Guitar Review* 12, 193–194.

Bellow, A. (1970). *The Illustrated History of the Guitar.* New York: Franco Colombo.

Brindle, R. S. (1975). *The New Music: The Avant-Garde Since 1945.* London: Oxford University Press.

Chew, G. (1980). "Song." In *The New Grove Dictionary of Music and Musicians*, edited by Stanley Sadie. Vol. 17, pp. 510–521. London: Macmillan.

Cogan, R., and Escot, P. (1976). *Sonic Design: The Nature of Sound and Music.* Cambridge MA: Publication Contact International.

Cohen, A. I. (1987). *International Encyclopedia of Women Composers.* 2d ed. New York: Books & Music.

Cunningham, M.; Stevenson, R.; and Larrea Palacín, A. (1980). "Spain." In *The New Grove Dictionary of Music and Musicians*, edited by Stanley Sadie. Vol. 17, pp. 784–805. London: Macmillan.

Drennen, M. (1975). Liner notes on *Music for Voice and Guitar* [LP]. New York: RCA Records.

Gilmore, G., and Pereira, M. (1976). *Guitar Music Index.* Honolulu HI: Galliard.

Griffiths, P. (1981). *Modern Music: The Avant-Garde Since 1945.* New York: George Braziller.

Heck, T. (1978a). "I lieder di Schubert per chitarra." *Il Fronimo* 6(24), 16–21.

_____. (1978b). "I lieder di Schubert per chitarra." *Il Fronimo* 6(25), 24–29.

Helleu, L. (198?). *"La guitarre en concert."* Paris: Éditions Musicales Transatlantiques.

Hunt, J. P. (1992). *Analyses of Music for Solo Voice and Percussion, 1950-1990.* Unpublished doctoral dissertation, Teachers College, Columbia University, New York.

Hurley, P. (1989a). "The Guitar in Song: An Introduction." *Soundboard* 16(2), 33–36.

_____. (1989b). "The Guitar in Song: An Introduction. Part II—Folk songs." *Soundboard,* 16(3), 21–25.

_____. (1989c). "The Guitar in Song: An Introduction. Part III—Songs before 1750." *Soundboard* 16(4), 39–43.

_____. (1990a). "The Guitar in Song: An Introduction. Part IV—The 19th Century." *Soundboard* 17(1), 43–48.

_____. (1990b). "The Guitar in Song: An Introduction. Part V—The 20th Century." *Soundboard* 17(2), 50–55.

Jape, M., ed. (1989). *Classical Guitar Music in Print.* Philadelphia: Musicdata.

Kingsley, V. (1951). "Songs with Guitar." *Guitar Review* 12, 180–181.

Libbert, J. (1981). "Lieder und gesänge mit gitarre." *Musica* 35(3), 250.

Lust, P. (1985). *American Vocal Chamber Music, 1945–1989: An Annotated Bibliography.* Westport CT: Greenwood.

Morton, B., and Collins, P., eds. (1992). *Contemporary Composers.* Chicago: St. James.

Moser, W. (1985). *Gitarre-musik—Ein internationaler katalog.* Hamburg: Joachim-Trekel-Verlag.

Noble, J. (1959). "Britten's 'Songs from the Chinese.'" *Tempo,* 52, 25-29.

Poulton, D. (1980). Vihuela. In *The New Grove Dictionary of Music and Musicians,* edited by Stanley Sadie. Vol. 19, pp. 757–761. London: Macmillan.

Randel, D. M., ed. (1986). *The New Harvard Dictionary of Music.* Cambridge MA: Belknap Press of Harvard University Press.

Rezits, J. (1983). *The Guitarist's Resource Guide: Guitar Music in Print and Books on the Art of Guitar.* Park Ridge IL: Pallma.

Rohr, J. (1982). "Guitar: Consort to the Voice. Chapter III—Hans Werner Henze: Kammermusik. *Guitar Review* 51, 15-24.

Schneider, J. (1985). *The Contemporary Guitar.* Berkeley: University of California Press.

Schwarz, W. (1984). *Guitar Bibliography—An International Listing of Theoretical Literature on Classical Guitar from the Beginning to the Present.* München: K. G. Saur.

Sclar, J. R. (1977). "Chapter I—Benjamin Britten: Songs from the Chinese." *Guitar Review* 42, 18-24.

_____. (1979). "Guitar: Consort to the Voice. Chapter II—Dominick Argento: Letters from Composers." *Guitar Review,* 45, 6-11.

Slonimsky, N., ed. (1978). *Baker's Biographical Dictionary of Musicians.* 6th ed. New York: Schirmer.

Smith, D., and Eagleson, L. (1990). *Guitar and Lute Music in Periodicals—An Index.* Berkeley CA: Fallen Leaf.

Stevens, D. (1960). *A History of Song.* London: Hutchinson.

Turnbull, H., and Heck, T. (1980). "Guitar." In *The New Grove Dictionary of Music and Musicians,* edited by Stanley Sadie. Vol. 7, pp. 825–843. London: Macmillan.

Wachsmann, K.; McKinnon, J. W.; Harwood, I.; and Poulton, D. (1980). "Lute." In *The New Grove Dictionary of Music and Musicians,* edited by Stanley Sadie. Vol. 11, pp. 342–365. London: Macmillan.

Wade, G. (1980). *Traditions of the Classical Guitar.* London: John Calder.

Wittlich, G. E., ed. (1975). *Aspects of Twentieth-Century Music.* Englewood Cliffs NJ: Prentice-Hall.

Zaimont, J. L., and Famera, K., eds. (1981). *Contemporary Concert Music by Women—A Directory of the Composers and Their Works.* Westport CT: Greenwood.

Appendix A
Publishers and Distributors

ACA

American Composers Alliance
170 West 74th St.
New York, NY 10023

Acoma

Acoma/Nambe Editions
PO Box 1261, Station K
Toronto
Ontario M4P 3E5
Canada

Agencji

Wydawnicto Muzyczne Agencji Autorkiej
ul. Hipoteczna 2
PL-00-092 Warszawa
Poland

Alpuerto

Editorial Alpuerto (U.S.—GSP)
Caños del Peral 7, 1º D.
28013 Madrid
Spain

AMC

American Music Center
30 West 26th St., Suite 1001
New York, NY 10010-2011

AMP

Associated Music Publishers (U.S.—GSP)
(see Leonard)

Andresier

Andresier Edition (U.S.—Brazinmukanta)
c/o Bardic Edition
6 Fairfax Crescent
Aylesbury
Buckinghamshire HP20 2ES
England

Anglian	Anglian Edition (specific address unknown) England
APNM	Association for the Promotion of New Music c/o Music Publishing Services 236 West 26th St., Suite 11S New York, NY 10001
Ariadne	Ariadne Buch- und Musikverlag GmbH Schottenfeldgaße 45 A-1070 Wien Austria
Arnaeus	Arnaeus Music PO Box 5376 N. Hollywood, CA 91616
Ashdown	Edwin Ashdown c/o Elkin Music International 16 NE 4th St. Ft. Lauderdale, FL 33301
Aureus	Aureus Publishing 144, Marlborough Rd. Cardiff CF2 5BZ, Wales England
Australia	Australian Music Centre PO Box N 690 Grosvenor Place Sydney 2000 Australia
Bastet	Bastet Productions The Couch House, Lysways Lane Longdon Green near Rugeley, WS15 4QB England
Beckenhorst	Beckenhorst Press 3821 North High St. PO Box 14273 Columbus, OH 43214

Belgium	Centre Belge de Documentation Musicale rue d'Arlon 75-77 B-1040 Bruxelles Belgium
Belwin	CPP/Belwin 15800 NW 48th Ave. Hialeah, FL 33014-6487
Ben Yar	Ben Yar Productions 300 West 108th St. New York, NY 10025 e-mail: yarmo4@aol.com
Berandol	Berandol Music, Ltd. c/o Ralph Cruickshank 1266 Minaki Rd. Mississauga Ontario L5G 2X4 Canada
Berben	Edizioni Musicali Berben (U.S.—Presser) Via Redipuglia 65 I-60122 Ancona Italy
Billaudot	Gérard Billaudot Éditeur 14, rue de l'Échiquier F-75010 Paris France
BKJ	BKJ Publications Box 377 Newton, MA 02161
Bommer	Druckerei Bommer GmbH Wallenburger Straße 40 D-83714 Miesbach Germany
Boosey	Boosey & Hawkes, Inc. 24 East 21st St. New York, NY 10010-7200

Borup	Edition A. Borup-Jørgensen v/ Elisabeth Selin Elme Allé 11, Hareskov DK-3500 Værløse Denmark
Bote	Bote & Bock GmbH & Co. (U.S.—Presser) Hardenbergstraße 9a D-10623 Berlin Germany
Brazilliance	Brazilliance Music (dist.—GSP) 4104 Witzel Dr. Sherman Oaks, CA 91423
Brazinmukanta	Brazinmukanta Publications Suite #108 73 Ireland Place Amityville, NY 11701
Breitkopf	Breitkopf & Härtel (U.S.—Broude & GSP) Walkmühlstraße 52 Postfach 1707 D-65007 Wiesbaden Germany
Broude	Alexander Broude, Inc. 575 Eighth Ave. New York, NY 10018
Brunton	Brunton Music (specific address unknown) England
Budapest	Editio Musica Budapest (U.S.—Boosey) PO Box 322 H-1370 Budapest Hungary
Canada	Canadian Music Centre Chalmers House 20 St. Joseph St. Toronto, Ontario M4Y 1J9 Canada

Casa	Casa de la Guitarra (U.S.—GSP) Shimo-Ochiai 3-17-49 Shinjuku-Ku Tokyo 161 Japan
Catalana	Catalana d'Ediciones Musicales (specific address unknown) Spain
Cavata	Cavata Music Publishers (see Presser)
Chanterelle	Chanterelle Verlag (U.S.—GSP) Postfach 103909 D-6900 Heidelberg Germany
Chester	Chester Music (U.S.—MMB & GSP) 8/8 Frith St. London W1V 5TZ England
Choudens	Éditions Choudens (U.S.—Presser) 38, rue Jean Mermoz F-75008 Paris France
CNY	CNY Publishers PO Box 4309 Tacoma, WA 98438
Colombo	Franco Colombo (see Belwin)
Columbia	Columbia Music (see Presser)
Creative	Creative Music Publishing 1560 W. Riverview St. Decatur, IL 62522
Crouch	Crouch Music 'Dassells' Priory Road Hastings East Sussex TN34 3JS England
Dim	Ediciones Musicales Dim (specific address unknown) Spain

Doberman	Les Éditions Doberman-Yppan (U.S.—GSP) C.P. 2021 St. Nicholas, Quebec G0S 3L0 Canada
Doblinger	Doblinger (U.S.—FMD) Postfach 882 Dorotheergasse 10 A-1011 Wien Austria
Donemus	Donemus Amsterdam (U.S.—Presser) Paulus Potterstraat 14 1071 CZ Amsterdam Netherlands
DVfM	Deutscher Verlag für Musik (U.S.—GSP) (see Breitkopf)
EAM	European American Music Distributors Corp. PO Box 850 Valley Forge, PA 19482
Egtved	Edition Egtved ApS (U.S.—EAM) PO Box 20 DK-6040 Egtved Denmark
Ehrling	Ehrlingförlagen Box 21133 S-100 31 Stockholm Sweden
English	English Guitar Centre Pavement Hill The Green Sheriff Hutton York YO6 1QB England
Engstrøm	Engstrøm & Sødring Musikforlag Borgergade 17 DK-1300 København K Denmark

Eschig

Éditions Max Eschig (U.S.—Presser)
215, rue de Faubourg Saint-Honoré
F-75008 Paris
France

Fazer

Fazer Musiikki Oy (U.S.—Presser)
Länsituulentie 1A
PL 169
SF-02101 Espoo
Finland

Feedback

Feedback Studio Verlag (U.S.—FMD)
Gentner Straße 23
D-5 Köln 1
Germany

Finland

Finnish Music Information Centre
Lauttasaarentie 1
FIN-00200 Helsinki
Finland

FMD

Foreign Music Distributors
13 Elkay Dr.
Chester, NY 10918

Foetisch

Foetisch SA
rue de Bourg 6
CH-1002 Lausanne
Switzerland

Gamber

Gamber Press
17 St. Peter's Grove
London W6 9AY
England

Gendai

The Gendai Guitar
1-16-14 Chihaya-cho
Toshima-ku
Tokyo 171
Japan

General

General Words & Music
c/o Neil Kjos Music Co.
4382 Jutland Dr.
Box 178270
San Diego, CA 92117

GSP

Guitar Solo Publications
1411 Clement St.
San Francisco, CA 94118

Guilys

Edition Guilys
(specific address unknown)
Switzerland

Gyldendal

Gyldendal Norsk Forlag
Sehedsteds Gate 4
Postboks 6860 St. Olavs Plass
N-0130 Oslo
Norway

Hansen

Edition Wilhelm Hansen AS (U.S.—MMB
& GSP)
Bornholmsgade 1
DK-1266 København K
Denmark

Helbling

Edition Helbling KG.
E. Harm & Co.
Kaplanstraße 9
Postfach 12
A-6063 Rum
Austria

Helvetia

Helvetia-Verlag & Bandproduktion
Gerhard Zießnitz
Kreuzbergstraße 7
D-10965 Berlin
Germany

Iceland

Iceland Music Information Centre
Sídumúli 34
108 Reykjavík
Iceland

Ione

Ione Press (see Schirmer)

Ireland

The Contemporary Music Centre
95 Lower Baggot St.
Dublin 2
Ireland

Kontrapunkt	Edition Kontrapunkt Slotsalleen 16 DK-2930 Klampenborg Denmark
Leonard	Hal Leonard Publishing Corp. 7777 West Bluemound Rd. Milwaukee, WI 53213
Margaux	Edition Margaux (U.S.—GSP) (see Neue)
Merion	Merion Music (see Presser)
Mills	Mills Music (U.S.—Leonard) 20 Denmark St. London England
MMB	MMB Music, Inc. Contemporary Arts Building 3526 Washington Ave. St. Louis, MO 63103-1019
Modern	Edition Modern (U.S.—GSP) Amalienstraße 40 D-76133 Karlsruhe Germany
Moeck	Edition Moeck (U.S.—EAM) Postfach 143 D-3100 Celle Germany
Möseler	Karl Heinrich Möseler Verlag (U.S.—MMB) Hoffman-von-Fallerslebenstraße 8-10 Postfach 1460 D-3340 Wolfenbüttel Germany
Müller	Müller & Schade AG Kramgasse 50 Postfach 715 CH-3000 Bern 7 Switzerland

Neue

Verlag Neue Musik
Köpenicker Straße 175
D-10997 Berlin
Germany

New Art

New Art Music Editions
799 Beach Ave.
Winnepeg, Manitoba
R2L 1E1
Canada

Norsk

Norsk Musikforlag AS
Karl Johansgaten 39
PO Box 1499 Vika
Oslo
Norway

Norway

Norwegian Music Information Centre
(Norsk Musikkinformasion)
Tollbugt. 28
N-0157 Oslo
Norway

Olivan

Olivan Press
(specific address unknown)
England

Opera

Opera Tres Ediciones Musicales (U.S.—GSP)
Apdo. de Coneos 18077
28080 Madrid
Spain

Orlando

Orlando-Musikverlag
Gartenmaier KG
Kaprunerstrße 11
D-80689 München
Germany

Orphée

Editions Orphée, Inc. (dist.—GSP)
407 North Grant Ave.
Suite 400
Columbus, OH 43215-2157

Oxford

Oxford University Press, Inc.
200 Madison Ave.
New York, NY 10016

Peer	Peer Music 810 Seventh Ave. New York, NY 10019
Peters	C.F. Peters Corp. 373 Park Ave. South New York, NY 10016
Pizzicato	Pizzicato Edizioni Musicali Via M. Ortigara 10 I-33100 Udine Italy
Preissler	Musikverlag Josef Preissler (U.S.—GSP) Postfach 521 Bräuhausstraße 8 D-8000 München 2 Germany
Presser	Theodore Presser Co. 1 Presser Place Bryn Mawr, PA 19010-3490
Primavera	Primavera Music 110 Wyatt Park Rd. Streatham London S.W.2 3TP England
Puerto Rico	Asociación Nacional de Compositores en Puerto Rico Rio Piedras, PR
Red House	Red House Editions Box 2123 Footscray Victoria 3011 Australia
Reimers	Edition Reimers (U.S.—Presser) Box 15030 S-161 15 Bromma-Stockholm Sweden
Reuter	Reuter & Reuter Förlags AB c/o Notservice Box 533 S-182 15 Danderyd Sweden

Ricordi	BMG Ricordi S.p.A. (U.S.—Boosey) Via Berchet, 2 I-20121 Milano Italy
Ricordi S.A.	Ricordi Americana S.A. (U.S.—Boosey & GSP) Cangallo, 1558 1037 Buenos Aires Argentina
Robitschek	Adolf Robitschek Musikverlag Graben 14 (Bräunerstraße 2) Postfach 42 A-1011 Wien Austria
Rodrigo	Ediciones Joaquin Rodrigo, S.A. (U.S.—GSP) General Yagüe, 11. 4°J 28020 Madrid Spain
Roeginga	Roeginga Edition 27, Dunedin Rd. Rainham, Essex. RM13 8HA England
Romero	Romero y Fernandez (specific address unknown)
Samfundet	Samfundet (U.S.—Peters) Gråbrødrestræde 18,1 DK-1156 København K Denmark
Santiago	Santiago de Compostela C/. Pablo Aranda 6 Madrid Spain
Schirmer	E.C. Schirmer Music Co. 138 Ipswich St. Boston, MA 02215-3534

Schott	Schott & Co. Ltd. (U.S.—EAM & GSP) 48 Great Marlborough Street London W1V 2BN England
Schott Japan	Schott Japan Co. Ltd. (U.S.—EAM & GSP) Kasuga Bldg. 2-9-3 Iadabashi Chiyoda-ku Tokyo 102 Japan
Scotland	Scottish Music Information Centre 1 Bowmont Gardens Glasgow G12 9LR Scotland
Seesaw	Seesaw Music Corp. 2067 Broadway New York, NY 10023
Sikorski	Hans Sikorski (U.S.—Leonard) Johnsallee 23 D-20148 Hamburg Germany
Sonzogno	Casa Musicale Sonzogno (U.S.—Presser) Via Bigli 11 I-20121 Milano Italy
Sounz	SOUNZ New Zealand PO Box 10042 Wellington New Zealand
Southern	Southern Music Co. PO Box 329 1100 Broadway San Antonio, TX 78292
Studio	Edition Studio Bruno Strobl Winkl 12 A-9701 Rothenthurn Austria

Supraphon	Bärenreiter Editio Supraphon (U.S.—FMD) Hudební nakladatelství 112 00 Praha 2, Chopinova 4 Czechoslovakia
Sweden	Swedish Music Information Centre Box 27327 S-102 54 Stockholm Sweden
Symphonia	Symphonia Verlag (specific address unknown) Switzerland
Tingluti	Tingluti Forlag Præstehusene 111 DK-2620 Albertslund Denmark
Tonger	P.J. Tonger, Musikverlag Postfach 50 18 18 D-50978 Köln Germany
Tonos	Tonos Musikverlag (U.S.—Seesaw & GSP) Ahastraße 9 D-64285 Darmstadt Germany
Trans	Éditions Musicales Transatlantiques (U.S.—Presser) 151-153, Avenue Jean-Jaurès F-75019 Paris France
Trekel	Joachim-Trekel-Verlag (U.S.—GSP) Postfach 620428 D-2000 Hamburg 62 Germany
Union	Union Musical Ediciones c/o Music Sales Corp. 5 Bellvale Rd. Chester, NY 10918 or Newmarket Rd. Bury St. Edmunds Suffolk IP33 3YB England

Universal	Universal Edition A.G. (U.S.—EAM) Postfach 3 A-1015 Wien Austria
Venezolanos	Musico Venezolanos Contemporaneos Instituto Latinamericano "Vincente Emilio Sojo" av. Los Mangos #9, Los Chorros Caracas 1071 Venezuela
Virtuoso	Virtuoso Editions c/o Soundspells Productions 86 Livingston St. Rhinebeck, NY 12572
Vogt	Musikverlag Vogt & Fritz (dist.—Zimmermann) Friedrich-Stein-Straße 10 D-97421 Schweinfurt Germany
Waiteata	Waiteata Press Music Editions (U.S.—Canada) School of Music Victoria University of Wellington PO Box 600 Wellington New Zealand
Waterloo	Waterloo Music Co., Ltd. (U.S.—GSP) 3 Regina St. North Waterloo, Ontario N2J 4A5 Canada
Weinberger	Josef Weinberger Ltd. 12-14 Mortimer St. London W1N 7RD England
Wheeler	Scott Wheeler Music 85 Haverhill St. North Reading, MA 01864 e-mail: swheeler@emerson.edu

Willis	Willis Music Co. 7380 Industrial Highway Florence, KY 41042
Woza	Woza Music 28 Park Gate, Blackheath London SE3 9XF England
Zanibon	G. Zanibon Edition (U.S.—Peters & GSP) Piazza dei Signori, 44 I-35100 Padova Italy
Zerboni	Edizioni Suvini Zerboni (U.S.—GSP) via M.F. Quintiliano 40 I-20138 Milano Italy
Zimmermann	Wilhelm Zimmermann, Musikverlag Bretzenheimerstraße 40 D-55128 Mainz Germany
Zindermans	Zindermans Music Publishing (specific address unknown) Göteburg Sweden

Appendix B
Composers of
Unpublished Works

David Adams

PO Box 1214
Box Hill Vic 3128
Australia

Zbigniew Bargielski

Kriehubergasse 25/10
A-1050 Wien
Austria

Carol Barnett

3722 Pleasant Ave. South
Minneapolis, MN 55409-1227

Garth Baxter

2744 Murkle Rd.
Westminster, MD 21158

Ivan Bellocq

La Concherie—Tilly
F-78790 Septeuil
France

Gilbert Biberian

49 Copt Elm Rd.
Cheltenham
GLOS. GL53 8AG
England

Herb Bielawa

81 Denslowe Dr.
San Francisco, CA 94132

Erling D. Bjerno

Morten Nielsensvej 4
DK-9200 Ålborg SV
Denmark

William Bland

15978 Shinham Rd.
Hagerstown, MD 21740

Christopher Bochmann	Escola Superior de Música de Lisboa Rua do Ataíde, 7-A 1200 Lisboa Portugal
Gilles Yves Bonneau	1202 E. Pike St., #656 Seattle, WA 98122
Jean-Yves Bosseur	6, rue Bellanger F-92200 Neuilly/S France
Alois Bröder	Grüner Weg 28 D-64285 Darmstadt Germany
Richard Charlton	Charlton Music PO Box 405 Edgecliff NSW 2027 Australia
Gian Paolo Chiti	Via Proba Petronia 82 I-00136 Roma Italy
Mogens Christensen	Asylplassen 13 N-5018 Bergen Norway
Henrik Colding-Jørgensen	Kildehuset 3, 3. TV. DK-2670 Greve Denmark
Paul Cooijmans	Postbus 44 5737 ZG Laarbeek Netherlands
Andrew Creaghan	PO Box 11211 Edmonton A.B. T5J 3K5 Canada
Allan Crossman	2185 Wilson Ave. #5 Montréal, Quebec H4A 2T4 Canada
Stephen Dembski	96 Perry St., Apt. B-22 New York, NY 10014

Marybel Dessagnes	26 rue des Soeurs Blanches F-74000 Annecy France
Gary Diaz	2550 Olinville Ave. #14B Bronx, NY 10467
Stephen Dodgson	4 Scarth Rd. London SW13 0ND England
David Farquhar	15 Nottingham St. Karori Wellington New Zealand
Jonathan Fitzgerald	c/o Southern Cross University Lismore Campus, PO Box 157 Lismore NSW 2480 Australia
Sheila Mary Forrester	1413 Stone Rd. Tallahassee, FL 32303
John Frandsen	Gl. Bregnerødvej 10 DK-3520 Farum Denmark
Stefan Fuchs	Tagensdorf 30 A-8083 St. Stefan / R Austria
Kay Gardner	Sea Gnomes Music PO Box 33 / Church St. Stonington, Maine 04681-0033
Eric Gross	54/84 St. Georges Crescent Drummoyne NSW 2047 Australia
Kevin Hiatt	2811 Coldstream Way, Apt. A Baltimore, MD 21234
Bjørn Hjelmborg	c/o Johan Hjelmborg Kastanievej 43 DK-2840 Holte Denmark

Ludger Hofmann-Engl	12 Essenden Rd. South Croydon London CR2 0BU England
Kay Holmquist	Sankt Pauli Kyrkogata 19 A 211 49 Malmö Sweden
Jerome Hughes	5 Short Hills Circle, Apt. 2B Millburn, NJ 07041
Hans Huyssen	Baaderstraße 53 D-80469 München Germany
Gérard Iglesia	36 rue Cavé F-75018 Paris France
Glenda Keam	3 Sylvan Valley Ave. Titirangi Auckland 1007 New Zealand
Daniel Kingman	600 Shangri Lane Sacramento, CA 95825
Michael Knopf	12 Cilento Close White Rock, Q 4868 Australia
Ernst Kölz	Garbergasse 14/12 A-1060 Wien Austria
Annette Kruisbrink	Vechstraat 123 8021 AW ZWOLLE The Netherlands
Augustin Kubizek	Schönburgstraße 13/27 A-1040 WIEN Austria
Jonathan Kulp	1919 Burton Dr., #101-B Austin, TX 78741-4237 kulp.jon@mail.utexas.edu

Noël Lee	4, villa Laugier F-75017 Paris France
Leonard Lehrman	10 Nob Hill Gate Roslyn, NY 11576
David Leisner	900 West End Ave., Apt. #12A New York, NY 10025
Christine McCombe	23 Miller St. North Fitzroy Victoria, 3068 Australia
Luis Morales Giácoman	c/Mesón de Paredes 29, 2º D. 28012 Madrid Spain
Piotr Moss	ul. Jana Pawla II 26 m 702 PL-00-133 Warszawa Poland
Daniel Nightingale	823 Almond St. Philadelphia, PA 19125
Helmer Nørgaard	120 Løjtoftevej DK-4900 Nakskov Denmark
David D. Norton	7279 South 2300 East Salt Lake City, UT 84121-3945
William Ortiz	Calle Jagüey D-43, El Plantío Toa Baja, PR 00949
Atanas Ourkouzounov	1, rue Baudelaire, Apt. 105 F-27000 Evreux France
Apostolos Paraskevas	41 Wright Ave. Medford, MA 02155
Robert Parris	3307 Cummings Lane Chevy Chase, MD 20815
Marie Pelletier	4299 Des Érables Montréal, Quebec H2H 2C6 Canada

Dr. Claire Polin	374 Baird Rd. Merion, PA 19066-1415
Werner Raditschnig	Scheibenweg 19 A-5020 Salzburg Austria
Jeff Raheb	415 9th St. #3 Brooklyn, NY 11215
Alain Michel Riou	28, rue de la Poterne F-45000 Orléans France
John Ritchie	2/12 Mansfield Ave. Christchurch 1 New Zealand
Wilfried Satke	Plankengasse 16 A-2700 Wiener Neustadt Austria
Mia Schmidt	Poststraße 5 D-79098 Freiburg Germany
David W. Solomons	9, Legh Court Northenden Rd. Sale, Cheshire M33 2SQ England
Andy Sundstrøm	Tokkekøbvej 50 DK-3450 Allerød Denmark
Craig Utting	104 Constable St. Newtown Wellington 2 New Zealand
Martin Vishnick	12, Watling St. St. Albans Herts AL1 2PX England
Lodewijk de Vocht	c/o Anne Ardui-de Vocht Kerkplein 9 2300 Turnhout Belgium

Gwyneth Walker	R.D. 2 Box 263
	Randolph, VT 05060
Ferdinand Weiss	Christalnigg-Gasse 11/2
	A-2500 Baden
	Suisse

Voice and Difficulty Index

References are to entry numbers. Numbers in **bold**
denote song cycles. Numbers in *italics* signify song groups

ALTO

Easy 16, 159,*199*, 225, 227, 234, 279, 281,
363, 382, 479, 481, 487, 500, 575;
Medium **86**, 232, *299*, *342*, 458, 476, 480,
482, 483, 484, 485, 488, 489, 507; Difficult 87, **90,110**, 117, 150, 177, *182*, 195, 196,
229, 230, 235, 268, 269, 278, **319**, **386**,
391, **395**, *419*, 420, **457**, 459, *503*, **545**;
Very Difficult 115, 169, *263*, 392, 422,
430.

BARITONE

Easy 7, 16, 17, 18, 19, 20, 23, 26, *95*, 102, 105,
134, 140, 141, 143, 158, 186, *212*, 216, *226*,
236, 250, *260*, 266, 272, 279, 281, *302*,
305, *308*, 339, *343*, *375*, 382, 383, 387,
441, 443, *460*, 500, 501, 502, 514, 520,
521, 526, 535, 543, 556, 566, 567, 572;
Medium 1, 9, *49*, *50*, 61, 70, **84**, 86, **88**,
96, 103, *106*, 107, 119, *163*, *165*, **170**, **175**,
197, 217, 220, 224, 231, 238, 239, 240,
241, *265*, *275*, *298*, *300*, *301*, *303*, *304*,
307, *309*, *316*, *317*, 323, *325*, *328*, *329*,
340, *342*, 364, *367*, **373**, *385*, 408, 435,
436, 437, *439*, 451, 454, 455, 458, **461**,
492, 531, *533*, 536, 537, *538*, *557*, 558,
560, *562*, *563*, 564, *568*, 569, 570, 571;
Difficult **4**, **28**, 58, 87, **90**, **101**, **110**, **111**,
114, 117, **130**, 138, *147*, 150, **162**, **164**, **174**,
177, *198*, **203**, 206, **208**, 229, 230, *246*,
249, *252*, 264, **267**, 276, *277*, 278, **280**,
293, *311*, **321**, **327**, 333, 372, 377, **395**,
406, **407**, 411, *412*, *418*, *419*, 420, *429*, 442,
444, 459, **462**, 486, **504**, 517, *519*, 539,
541, *546*, 559, *561*, 565; Very Difficult **76**,
82, *201*, **207**, **209**, 218, *245*, **258**, **259**, **261**,
263, 283, 313, 314, **397**, 421, **427**, 430,
434, **473**, *478*, *498*, 524, 555, 573, 574.

BASS

Easy 16, 79, *199*, 225, 227, 234, 279, 281,
363, 382, 500, 575; Medium **86**, *139*, *202*,
232, *299*, *342*, 458, 476, 482, 489, 507;
Difficult **71**, 87, **90**, **110**, 117, 150, 177, 229,
230, 235, 268, 278, **319**, **395**, *419*, 420,
442, **457**, 459, 486, *503*; Very Difficult **31**,
263, 430.

MEZZO

Easy 7, 16, 17, 18, 19, 20, 23, 26, 36, *89*, *95*,
102, 105, 134, 140, 141, 143, 158, 159, 186,
200, *212*, 216, *226*, 236, 250, *260*, 266,
272, 279, 281, *302*, *305*, *308*, 339, *343*,
375, 382, 383, 387, *441*, 443, *460*, 500,
501, 502, 514, 520, 521, 526, 535, 543,
556, 566, 567, 572; Medium 1, 9, 37, *50*,
61, 70, **84**, 86, *96*, 97, 103, *106*, 107, 119,
163, *165*, **170**, 197, 217, 220, 224, 231, 238,
239, 240, 241, *265*, *275*, *298*, *300*, *301*,
303, *304*, *307*, *309*, *316*, *317*, *322*, 323,
325, *328*, *329*, 338, *340*, *342*, 364, *367*,
373, *385*, 408, 435, 436, 437, *439*, 451,
454, 455, 458, **461**, *499*, 530, 531, 536,
537, *557*, 558, *560*, *562*, *563*, 564, *568*,
569, 570, 571; Difficult **4**, **38**, 47, 55, 58,
69, 81, 87, 85, **90**, **101**, **110**, 114, 117, *120*,
123, **130**, 138, *147*, 150, **162**, **168**, **174**, 177,
187, *198*, **203**, 206, **208**, *210*, **211**, 229,
230, **249**, 251, *252*, 262, 264, 276, *277*,
278, **280**, *293*, *311*, **321**, **336**, **371**, 372,
374, *376*, 377, **386**, **388**, *394*, **395**, **406**,
407, 411, *412*, *418*, *419*, 420, *429*, 444, 459,
462, 496, **504**, *512*, 517, *519*, *541*, *546*,
559, *561*, 565; Very Difficult *33*, *73*, **76**,
82, **133**, **137**, 169, **192**, 218, *245*, **258**, *263*,
283, 314, 349, **380**, **410**, 430, 431, 432,
434, 463, **473**, *478*, **497**, *498*, 573, 574.

SOPRANO

Easy 16, 17, 18, 19, *30*, 144, 151, 155, 215,
250, 281, 282, *288, 305, 308, 343,* 354,
393, 409, 449, 466, *467, 468,* 500, 522,
527, 529, 532, 556, 566, 567; Medium 6,
10, 21, 22, 24, 25, *32,* 34, 40, 41, *42, 43,*
44, 45, 51, 52, *54,* 56, 64, 65, *67, 78, 91,*
92, **112,** 122, *124,* 125, 126, *152, 154,* **156,**
160, 161, 173, 176, **179,** *184, 213,* 214, 221,
222, 223, *287, 289,* 292, *307, 309,* 310,
325, 351, 423, *438, 440,* 450, 453, 465,
469, *470,* 508, *509, 510, 515,* 516, 523,
534, 547, 550, 553, *557,* 558, *562, 563,*
564, *568,* 570, **576;** Difficult 8, *12, 13,* **14,**
15, 29, **35,** *39,* **46,** 47, 48, 55, **57, 59,** *60,*
63, 87, **90, 93,** 98, *99, 100,* 104, **108, 109,**
110, 113, 117, **127, 128, 129, 130,** 135, *136,*
138, *145,* **146, 149,** 150, **153, 157, 167,**
171, 172, 177, **181, 185,** 190, *205,* 219,
229, 230, 237, **254,** 264, *273,* 278, **280,**
284, **285,** 286, 290, 291, *294,* 312, **315,**
318, 320, *332,* 337, **334,** *350,* **352, 353,**
355, 356, **357, 358,** 359, **360,** 361, 362,
365, *369,* **374,** *379,* **386,** *390,* **395,** 396,
413, 417, 419, 420, 424, 425, 426, *433,*
444, 452, *456,* **471, 474,** 475, **477,** *491,*
511, 525, 528, *541, 544,* 548, 549, 552,
559, *561,* 565; Very Difficult **2,** *3,* 5, *11,*
53, *72,* 74, *80, 94,* 116, *118,* 121, 131, 132,
148, *166,* 169, *180,* **183,** *188,* **189,** 191, 193,
204, 242, *244,* **255, 274, 296,** *306,* 331,
335, 341, *345,* 349, **368,** 381, **384,** 404,
405, **414,** *415, 416,* **428,** *445,* 446, 447,

448, 472, *490,* **505,** 513, 551, 554, 573,
574.

TENOR

Easy 16, 17, 18, 19, *30,* 144, 151, 155, 250,
281, *288, 305, 308, 343,* 346, 354, 398,
401, 402, 403, 409, 449, 466, *467, 468,*
500, 522, 527, 529, 532, 556, 566, 567;
Medium 6, *10, 21,* 22, 24, 25, *32, 43,* 45,
51, 52, *54,* 64, 65, *67,* **88,** *91,* 92, 97, 125,
126, **142,** *152, 154,* **156,** *160, 161, 173, 184,*
194, *213,* 221, 222, 223, 257, 271, *287,*
292, *307, 309,* 310, 324, *325,* **326,** 347,
348, *351,* 400, *438, 440,* 450, 453, 464,
465, **469,** *470, 493,* 508, *509, 515,* 516,
523, 534, 547, 550, 553, *557,* 558, *562,*
563, 564, *568,* 570, **576;** Difficult 8, *12,*
13, 48, **59,** *60, 62,* **63,** 66, *68,* 75, **83,** 87,
90, 93, 101, **108, 109, 110,** 117, **127, 128,**
129, 130, *136,* 138, *145,* **146, 149,** 150, **153,**
167, *171,* 177, **181, 185,** 190, *205,* 219, *228,*
229, 230, 233, 237, **253,** *256,* 264, 270,
278, **280,** 284, **285,** 290, *294,* 312, **315,**
320, *332,* 337, **352, 353,** *379,* 389, *390,*
395, 399, *413, 419,* 420, 424, 425, 426,
433, 442, 444, 452, *456,* **471, 474, 477,**
511, **518, 540,** *541,* **542,** *544,* 548, 552,
559, *561,* 565; Very Difficult *11,* 27, **53,**
77, 131, 132, *188,* **189, 243,** *244,* **247,** *248,*
295, 296, 297, 330, 341, **344,** *345, 366,*
370, **378, 384, 428,** 446, 447, *448, 490,*
494, 554, 573, 574.

General Index

References are to entry numbers except where specified "page"

Studio (publisher) 497
Suckling, Sir John 248, 547
Suite nach Altpolnischen Melodien 52
Sumer is icumen in 485
Supraphon (publisher) 158
Sur les Routes de Fer 150
Swan Songs 174
Sweden (publisher) 75, 168, 180, 190, 193,
    202, 203, 208, 212, 219, 220–224, 264,
    307–309, 332, 491
Swedish, works in 98, 168, 180, 190, 193,
    202, 203, 212, 219–224, 254, 264, 266,
    307–309, 328, 329, 341, 366, 427, 491,
    496
Symphonia (publisher) 22, 26

*Tabulaturen etlicher Lobgesang und Lied-
    lin* page 4
Tagore, Rabindranath 318
Tagwache 115
Tangents CSB 177
La Tarde sobre los Tejados 551
Tarditi, Orazio page 7
Tavole per Orfeo 380
Teasdale, Sara 42, 232
The Tempest 185
Ten Liebeslieder 289
Tennyson, Alfred, Lord 382
Tenori e contrabassi intabulati... page 4
Teryan, Vahan 488
13 Heine-Lieder 87
13 Prosodier 376
13 x von Tieren Singen 460
This Aye Neet 532
Thomas, Edward 253
Thomas, Tony 67
Three American Folk Songs 375
Three Argentine Popular Songs 32
Three Devotional Miniatures 176
Three from Sara 42
3 Gammelkinesiske Digte 81
Three Greek Songs 429
Three Herrick Songs 546
Three Lyrics 388
Three Madrigals 43
Three Pastorales 510
Three Poems by Stephen Crane 213
Three Poems of James Joyce 293
Three Shakespeare Songs 544
Three Songs 39, 97, 340
Three Songs for Baritone and Guitar 538
Three Songs for Countertenor 182
Three Songs from Shakespeare 311
Three Songs from the Hidden Words 277
Three Songs with Guitar 448
Thrilling, Isobel 531
Tidernes Følge 71

Tierverse von Bertolt Brecht 138
Tijl-Liederen 533
Times Three 235
Tingluti (publisher) 500
Tio Visor 329
Tippett, Michael page 1
To Hansum Dikt 99
To the Guitarists 237
Tonger (publisher) 248
Tonos (publisher) 90
Torben, Til 71
Towards Anthony Holborne 395
Trans (publisher) 351
Tre Canti 11
Tre Frammenti di Saffo 417
Tre Medititiva Sånger 491
Tre Sånger till Gitarr 190
Trekel (publisher) 283, 444
Tres Canciones Españolas 438
Tres Canciones para Niños 294
Tres Villancicos 439
Treue 20
Trofimowitz, Ingrid von 254
Trois Chanson Tristes 511
Trois Chansons 394
Trois Chants de Joie et de Soucis 351
Trois Complaintes 78
Trois Mélodies 120
Trois Sonnets de Louise Labé 82
Tromboncini, Bartolomeo page 4
Troubador songs 147
Troubadours page 3, page 4
Tu Fu 129
Tunström, Göran 202
Twelfth Night 323, 324
2 Dagsedlar 212
Two Ballads 512
Two Bookes of Aires 182
Two Love Poems 332
Two Motets 178
Two Old French Songs 519
Two Poems of Manley Hopkins 478
Two Remembrances 44
Two Rilke Songs 165
Two Sapphic Songs 200
2 Songs 73
Two Songs 3
2 Songs by Keats 118
Two Spanish Folksongs 30
Two Spanish Songs 273

Über Selbstkritik 402
Ubunzima (Misfortune) 426
Det Ulde Kor og Andre Dikte 99
Ulysses 291
...und die Liebe braucht ein Dach 20, 134,
    140, 141, 346, 347, 348, 443, 464–466